TWENTIETH CENTURY
INTERPRETATIONS
MAYNARD MACK, *Series Editor*
Yale University

NOW AVAILABLE
Collections of Critical Essays
ON

THE ADVENTURES OF HUCKLEBERRY FINN

ALL FOR LOVE

THE FROGS

THE GREAT GATSBY

HAMLET

HENRY V

THE ICEMAN COMETH

SAMSON AGONISTES

THE SOUND AND THE FURY

TWELFTH NIGHT

TWENTIETH CENTURY INTERPRETATIONS
OF

WALDEN

TWENTIETH CENTURY INTERPRETATIONS
OF

W A L D E N

A Collection of Critical Essays

Edited by

RICHARD RULAND

Prentice-Hall, Inc.   A SPECTRUM BOOK   *Englewood Cliffs, N. J.*

For M. A.

Contents

Introduction, *by Richard Ruland*   1

PART ONE—*View Points*

Gray Burr   7

John Dewey   8

Robert Frost   8

Perry Miller   9

Paul Lauter   10

Douglas Grant   11

Sherman Paul   12

Bruce King   15

Gerry Brenner   19

Constance Rourke   21

Frank Davidson   22

William Bysshe Stein   25

PART TWO—*Essays*

A Slight Sound at Evening, *by E. B. White*   27

The Intellectual Heritage of Thoreau,
   by Norman Foerster   34

The Organic Structure of *Walden,*
   by F. O. Matthiessen   50

The Movement of Thoreau's Prose,
   by John C. Broderick   64

Paradox in *Walden, by Joseph J. Moldenhauer*   73

The Religion of "Higher Laws," *by John B. Pickard*   85

Ancient Rites at Walden, *by Reginald L. Cook*   93

Transcendental Pastoral, *by Leo Marx*   101

Henry Thoreau, *by E. B. White*   113

Chronology of Important Dates   *115*
Notes on the Editor and Contributors   *117*
Selected Bibliography   *119*

Introduction

by Richard Ruland

Much has been written about Thoreau during the past fifty years, but little in the extensive bibliographies helps us understand his writing. Lewis Leary remarked in 1956 that Thoreau has long been at the mercy of "good hearted friends, of his own or later generations, who speak with more enthusiasm than judgment. He has been used too often as a rallier of causes. His prickly character has attracted partisans, so that he has been attacked by people who did not like him, his way of life or his ideas, or who did not like his friends or his friends' enthusiasms. Almost everyone who has written about Thoreau has attempted to prove something—that he was a hermit or not a hermit, a naturalist or a humanist, a scientist or a poet, a warm man disappointed in love or a cold man for whom love in the ordinary sense had no meaning." [1]

Certainly a good four-fifths of the writing on Thoreau is either undiscriminating appreciation or sentimental testimonial. Only a fraction of it focuses on his books and essays. In this respect Thoreau has shared the fate of many American authors who have come in for fresh assessment during the second and third decades of this century—the man and his writing have seemed less important than the support they could lend to the presuppositions of the critic studying them.

This is not to say that *Walden,* for instance, has been persistently misread. *Walden* has suffered most from tendentious and partial readings. It has a huge audience among lovers of bird and bush. With the essay on *Civil Disobedience,* it appears almost daily in manifestoes urging resignation from a world we never made. Like Emerson's *Essays, Walden* can even bring dreams of simplicity and self-reliance to the businessman seeking to clear his desk and maximize his profits. Because they are partial and incomplete, such readings diminish Thoreau's achievement and the greatness of his book—a book whose full quality we are only beginning to record a hundred years after

[1] Lewis Leary, "Thoreau," *Eight American Authors* (New York: The Modern Language Association of America, 1956), p. 157. Sherman Paul reached much the same conclusion five years later in the Introduction to *Thoreau: A Collection of Critical Essays* (Englewood Cliffs, N.J.: Prentice-Hall, Inc., 1962).

1

publication. It was not until F. O. Matthiessen's *American Renaissance* in 1941, most modern commentators agree, that the first effort was made to see *Walden* whole, to treat it as a book with a carefully planned, organically developed structure and not as a random group of essays composed of equally random, glittering aphorisms.

Thus the first requisite of a complete reading is to recognize that *Walden* is a carefully articulated, full-length book. Once we agree that its various parts contribute to a total statement, the way is clear for the kind of specialized study included in the present collection. For the essay which examines the style, the structure, or the imagery of *Walden* escapes the weakness of earlier readings to the extent that it stresses elements which serve the book as a whole. We have come only recently to this architectural approach, and there are as yet very few competent studies of the features which make *Walden* great. Whole areas are still imperfectly understood. Careful readers will agree, for example, that *Walden* is a very funny book (though many admirers doubtless greet this view with surprise or even dismay); yet there is not a single essay which deals successfully with the nature of Thoreau's wit or the intricate way it functions in *Walden*. The shades of wit and irony play an integral part in the workings of the book, and a ripe sensitivity to the location of Thoreau's tongue rather far up in his cheek (as one critic put it) is as essential to our reading of this author as it is to, say, Mark Twain. It will help us grasp, for one thing, the special nature of our narrator, the *persona* of Henry Thoreau at Walden Pond, who is not quite the same Henry Thoreau who has now built not a cabin but a book.

If there are as yet very few readings of *Walden* which are in any sense complete, it is not simply because we have been blind to the functioning of its parts. We often fail, as well, to recognize its nature. Reading it entirely as spiritual exploration may be more sophisticated, but is certainly no more complete than reading it as a manual of woodlore or social criticism. Thoreau was a poet to the marrow of his being, despite the fact that he wrote very few good verses. He was a poet because he approached language and the building of a book the way great poets do. He took the concrete details of his stay at Walden Pond and transformed them into a scriptural parable. Hence for the sensitive reader, *Walden is* an experience as well as a description of one. Thoreau insists that we learn from him, and yet he rejects any attempt on our part to follow his particular path from cabin to pond. He had his cabin and his pond; we have *Walden*.

It is not surprising that Thoreau's first readers misunderstood his book. His neighbors in Concord knew him well as the Henry Thoreau who had graduated from Harvard in 1837 and returned to live in his native village. They knew him as a young man who loved the woods and countryside (and who had by chance almost burned down a good stand of forest). They knew him as a taciturn, independent lad who lost a teaching post because he would not follow the rules and administer disciplinary punishment, who made a "perfect" pencil in the family factory and then abandoned the work because he had no desire to make another. They knew him as a handyman and surveyor, happy to work for a sufficiency and then resume his roaming through the neighborhood marshes, fields, and woodlots. Most of all they knew him as the devoted disciple of Emerson. Thoreau moved into Emerson's house in 1841. It was Emerson who published his "The Natural History of Massachusetts" in the *Dial*, and when Henry began building a cabin on Emerson's fourteen acres at nearby Walden Pond, there were doubtless many who recalled Emerson's "Self-Reliance" of 1841. "In the pleasing contrite wood-life which God allows me," Emerson had said, "let me record day by day my honest thought without prospect or retrospect, and I cannot doubt it will be found symmetrical, though I mean it not and see it not. My book should smell of pines and resound with the hum of insects."

It seemed to Thoreau's contemporaries that he walked in the shadow of Emerson's originality. Later critics have been satisfied to grant Emerson the genius of conception and Thoreau the initiative of action, but this easy dichotomy ignores the artistry of Thoreau's writing. Emerson's words in "Self-Reliance" are not an adequate description of *Walden*. Neither is his poem, "The Apology" (1846), although this too must have seemed at the time a seed sufficient to explain Thoreau's book:

> Think me not unkind and rude
>   That I walk alone in grove and glen;
> I go to the god of the wood
>   To fetch his word to men.
>
> Tax not my sloth that I
>   Fold my arms beside the brook;
> Each cloud that floated in the sky
>   Writes a letter in my book.
>
> Chide me not, laborious band,
>   For the idle flowers I brought;
> Every aster in my hand
>   Goes home loaded with a thought.
>
> There was never mystery
>   But 't is figured in the flowers;

Was never secret history
    But birds tell it in the bowers.

One harvest from thy field
    Homeward brought the oxen strong;
A second crop thine acres yield
    Which I gather in a song.

While either statement by Emerson might have suggested Thoreau's experiment—although there had been other retreats to the woods to serve as precedent—the stanzas above reveal as clearly as anything can the superiority of Thoreau's art. Emerson is limited here by his own poetics. He saw poetry as "meter-making argument" and accordingly produced nothing more than a rhymed apology for his daydreaming—an apology, incidentally, based on the plea that he too is really working hard. As a poet, he does little more than point to the raw materials which Thoreau's resilient prose was to raise to a far higher level of poetic art. Emerson talks about an action that Thoreau permits us to share.

These two passages from Emerson suggest fairly accurately what Thoreau's neighbors saw in *Walden* and what many readers of its 133 editions (by 1953) have also seen—when they have not read it as the record of an experiment in subsistence living. The local townspeople plagued Thoreau with questions about his adventure. What did he do? Did he get lonely? Many took his withdrawal so literally that he turned their misunderstanding against them when he framed the early pages of his book. Curiosity about the details of his experiment even impelled him to write and deliver a lecture on the subject. When *Walden* was published, some seven years after Thoreau left Walden Pond, he gave it the subtitle, Life in the Woods. He soon saw that this was a mistake and had the subtitle dropped, for the readers both of his day and ours invariably responded to "Woods" and ignored "Life." From the first, Thoreau meant to stress the life-discovering purpose of his sojourn.

As he labored over his notes and the successive versions of *Walden*, the book steadily became less limited to the specific time and place of his adventure in the woods. The concrete details of his experience, lifted from the journal pages and carefully set into the flow of his prose, lost the close tie they had had with an experiment in living conducted several years before. Thoreau the naturalist and Thoreau the transcendental scout reporting from the bush all but disappeared before an artist exercising the most precise tonal and structural control.[2] As a result, we cannot take the simplest word in *Walden* for

---

[2] For a thorough study of Thoreau's revisions, see James Lyndon Shanley, *The Making of Walden* (Chicago: The University of Chicago Press, 1957).

granted. The "I" we meet on the first page is Henry Thoreau the woodsman, the student of society and of his own soul, but it is also Henry Thoreau the artist, manipulating and coloring the experience of the woodsman in ways the earlier Henry could hardly have anticipated. It is further the window through which the writer hopes to glimpse the eternal, the Emersonian "eye" he offers to anyone sharing his curiosity. We look through this "I" as Thoreau looked through his pond—which is indeed a pond but also a mirror to the depths of the soul (this too, he hints, may be bottomless) and to the endless reaches of the heavens overhead. What is more, we come eventually to see that everything Thoreau claims for his pond he claims as well for his book. Our gaze is not true until we recognize Walden Pond itself lying between the covers of *Walden.*

The readers Thoreau had hoped to reach did not appreciate his efforts, and he was not successful in selling his two books. He had labored over *A Week on the Concord and Merrimac Rivers* while at Walden Pond. The only other book published during his lifetime, *A Week* appeared between covers largely at his own expense. After four years, he was forced to undertake storage of the remaining 706 copies—from an edition of 1000. "The wares are sent to me at last," he noted in 1853, "and I have an opportunity to examine my purchase. They are something more substantial than fame, as my back knows, which has borne them up two flights of stairs to a place similar to that to which they trace their origin. . . . I have now a library of nearly nine hundred volumes, over seven hundred of which I wrote myself. Is it not well that the author should behold the fruits of his labor?" J. L. Shanley is probably right to relate the artistic triumph of *Walden* to the commercial failure of *A Week.* Thoreau was in no position to underwrite the publication of his second book. During the years it took him to find support he went on reading sections to his friends and rearranging passages to heighten their effect. In the book which gradually took shape, the materials of memory were so transformed by imagination that they became parable, what Thoreau himself would call "scripture." His neighbors would certainly have seen presumption—and probably blasphemy—in his desire to create such a scripture, just as they balked (he knew they would) at his familiar reference to the Bible as an "old book" and his assumption that it in no way differed from the Vedas.

Walden is best understood as such a scriptural parable in which the simple narrative is persistently lifted and re-directed by the context Thoreau provides. Part of this context lies in the *persona* of the narrator, in the complex way his voice colors the details of his story with an irony that doubles the freight of his statement or with a wit that moves us instantly from beachcomber and camper to sage. An equally important part of that context, however, is the role Thoreau assigns his readers. Most of us, he concedes, are like John Farmer. We have commitments and responsibilities which make the path to Walden Pond inaccessible. But that path was solely for Thoreau's use anyway. He insists that it is not for us, and he abandoned it himself when it became too familiar to serve its purpose. Thoreau asks only that, like John Farmer, we long for renewal. He urges us to join John Farmer in the appropriate cleansing rituals and to allow ourselves peace to hear the sound of the flute. For although Thoreau marked no trail for us to follow, he did, in fact, play the flute. It is as the sound of his flute that he offers *Walden*. Everyone, he implies, must visit Walden Pond. Because it achieves the existential autonomy of poetry, his book provides an opportunity to do just that.

*   *   *

The essays which follow will speak for themselves. I have not sought representative samples of Thoreau criticism so much as a selection of complementary analyses. Taken as a more or less coherent statement, the anthology points the direction a fruitful reading of *Walden* might take.

R.R.

St. Louis
October, 1967

PART ONE

View Points

Gray Burr

THE ONE AND ONLY

He heard the flicker drumming in the wood,
It sounded different. He began to march
In a route step nobody understood.
Oh, Emerson, perhaps, with half an eye
Cocked upward and the other fixed in starch,
Caught glimpses of him as he shambled by.

He did a lot of travelling in Concord,
Mapping his progress as he went along,
Finding a pond an ocean unexplored,
Two rivers that were never truly charted,
A stretch of beach the surveys had all wrong:
Where standard maps left off, his atlas started.

Leaving to sheep their skins, to towns their ways,
He built a school because he felt perplexed;
Enrolled, and stayed there just as many days
As needed for a general education.
First he learned, and then he wrote the text.
Next term the course was open to the nation.

Many have applied but few have finished.
And none has ever quite achieved his rank.
Originals in our day have diminished,
Are frowned on rather, knocked about, and cut.
For luck like this, Thoreau would have them thank
Whatever gods have jarred them from the rut.

John Dewey

My knowledge of Thoreau has always been penumbral and in spite of the fact that the penumbra was of the quality of a halo, it never induced me to go further. . . . What holds of myself is true I imagine of many; they know indirectly enough about *Walden* of a general sort so they aren't moved to go into actual contact. . . . I am wondering why I have never gone to the sources in his case. Has he been presented with too much austerity—as a kind of The Last Puritan? I'm only asking.

Letter to Walter Harding, November 28, 1949 [1]

Robert Frost

Far be it from me . . . to regret that all the poetry isn't in verse. I'm sure I'm glad of all the unversified poetry of *Walden*—and not merely the nature-descriptive, but narrative as in the chapter on the play with the loon on the lake, and character-descriptive as in the beautiful passage about the French-Canadian woodchopper. That last alone with some things in Turgenieff must have had a good deal to do with the making of me.

Letter to Walter Prichard Eaton, July 15, 1915.

In one book . . . he surpasses everything we have had in America.

Letter to Wade Van Dore, June 24, 1922 [2]

A man may write well and very well all his life, yet only once in a lifetime have such luck with him in the choice of a subject—a real gatherer, to which everything in him comes tumbling. Thoreau's immortality may hang by a single book, but the book includes even his writing that is *not* in it. Nothing he ever said but sounds like a quotation from it. Think of the success of a man's pulling himself together under one one-word title. Enviable! [3]

[1] From *The Thoreau Society Bulletin*, XXX (January, 1950), 1. Reprinted by permission of *The Thoreau Society Bulletin*.

[2] Both letters are from "Frost and Thoreau," by Lawrence Thompson. From *The Thoreau Society Bulletin*, LXXXVIII (Summer, 1964), 4. Reprinted by permission of the author and *The Thoreau Society Bulletin*.

[3] *The Listener*, LII (August 26, 1954), 319.

Perry Miller

. . . *Walden* is one of the supreme achievements of the Romantic Movement—or to speak accurately, of Romantic Naturalism. . . . It is a magnificent autobiography, faithful in every detail to the setting, arising to the level of a treatise on imagination and taste, and all this without ever becoming didactic. When seen in such a perspective, it can be placed beside *The Prelude*. It is the "growth of a poet's mind," and despite all its wealth of concrete imagery it is centered not upon Nature, but upon Nature's brother, the intelligence of the artist. . . .

If the twentieth-century judgment of the Romantic aesthetic is correct, then Henry Thoreau is one of its monumental failures and martyrs, along with Shelley and Novalis. Neither he nor they were able to answer the terrible question of whether, once they committed themselves to the proposition that their most delicate experience was typified in Nature, they were thereafter actually writing about Nature —about Walden Pond, for instance—or about nothing more than their delicious experiences. If in reality they were only projecting their emotions onto the Natural setting, if the phoebes do not weep for human miseries, then their effort to find someone additional to themselves was doomed to ghastly defeat. In this view, the career of Henry Thoreau is as tragic as that of King Lear. He too sacrificed himself needlessly to a delusion.

In his first organized statement, Thoreau could say, with all the confidence that a Lear had in the love of his daughters, that when he detects a beauty in any recess of Nature he is reminded of the inexpressible privacy of a life, that he may rest content with nothing more than the sight and the sound. On the premise of that doctrine, he may properly say no more than "I am affected by the sight of the cabins of muskrats," or than "I am the wiser in respect to all knowledges, and better qualified for all fortunes, for knowing that there is a minnow in the brook." In the glowing confidence of these aphorisms lurks the assumption that moral law and natural law contain analogies, and that for this reason the writer may safely record facts without metaphors, since truths are bound to sprout from them. The later portions of Thoreau's *Journal*, those after 1854, with their tedious recordings of mere observations, of measurements, of statistics, seem

An excerpt from "Thoreau in the Context of International Romanticism." From The New England Quarterly, *XXXIV (June, 1961), 156-59. Copyright © 1961 by* The New England Quarterly. *Reprinted by permission of the publisher.*

to attest not only the dwindling of his vitality but the exhaustion of the theory upon which he commenced to be an author in the first place. He immolated himself on the pyre of an untenable concept of literary creation.

And yet, he refuses to be consumed. Expound *Walden,* if you will, as a temporary and so an empty triumph of the Romantic dream, as a work doomed to diminish with the recession of that dream, yet the book refuses to go into the archeological oblivion of, shall I say? Shelley's *The Revolt of Islam.* . . . The obvious answer, or rather the easy one, is that Thoreau was a great writer, and so his pages survive in spite of changes in metaphysical fashions. But that is truly an easy, a luxurious way of salvaging our poet. The more difficult, but I believe the more honest and, in the final accounting, the more laudatory way is to say that the Romantic balance, or its "Idea" of combination, of fusing the fact and the idea, the specific and the general, is still a challenge to the mind and to the artist. Thoreau was *both* a Transcendentalist and a Natural Historian. He never surrendered on either front, though the last years of the *Journal* show how desperate was the effort to keep both standards aloft. He said, in the central conceptual passage of *Walden,* that he wanted to drive life into a corner, to publish its meanness if it proved to be mean, but that if it should turn out to be sublime, then to give a true account of its sublimity. "The universe constantly and obediently answers to our conceptions" was his resolute determination. For what more sublime a cause, even though it be a questionable thesis, can a man expend himself?

Paul Lauter

The dramatic quality of the symbolic act . . . makes it ideal matter for literary development. . . . It is surely no accident that most of Thoreau's important works—e.g., *A Week,* "Civil Disobedience," *Walden*—arise from concrete experiences that he has deliberately set up, and specifically presented, as symbolic testimonies of action. These symbolic acts—launching himself on the Concord River, refusing his tax, moving to Walden—have, aside from the literary works which arise from them, inherent value as challenging testimonies. They confront us with things done, with dramatic engagements from which

An excerpt from "Thoreau's Prophetic Testimony," by Paul Lauter. From Thoreau in Our Season *in* The Massachusetts Review, *IV (1962-63), 116-17. Copyright © 1962, 1966 by the University of Massachusetts Press. Reprinted by permission of the publisher.*

we can hardly escape, and for which we must then attempt some explanation, if only to satisfy our own impatience with them. But they are also of value to Thoreau because a gospel can be constructed from them, a gospel in which the reader's responses, even, or perhaps especially, his irritation, can be used to extend the reverberations of the acts, to focus their significance, to recommend their points to the reader.

Douglas Grant

As a tract in economics, *Walden,* Thoreau's account of his life in the woods, is absurd. A diet of beans and molasses may provide an individual with energy sufficient for all creditable activities, but a community which adopted beans and beets as the best idea for agriculture would rapidly sink to the condition of those peoples whose expression horrifies us today as they stare down accusingly on our affluent streets from posters appealing for famine relief. Life in the Congo will not be convenient for philosophers until there are the jungle equivalents of Concord and its railroad. But Thoreau never intended such an absurdity. His description of how he kept himself alive physically, like his mock statement of accounts showing that beans not eaten can be sold for profit, is intended to prepare his readers to receive two truths which bear sharply on the whole economy of human life. The first is that 'a man is rich in proportion to the number of things which he can afford to let alone,' and the other, that 'the cost of a thing is the amount of what I will call life which is required to be exchanged for it, immediately or in the long run.' Judging by these standards, he indicted society as poor and expensive; and it has not grown richer and cheaper since he wrote.

*   *   *

Some must work in the fields, Thoreau asserted, 'if only for the sake of tropes and expression.' Thoreau has been criticized from time to time as an observer of nature. He failed to distinguish some kinds of pine; he overlooked the commonest flower for so many years that he held it a rarity; he described the plumes of an ordinary bird of passage but could not name it. These would be faults if his business was plain facts and not 'tropes and expression.' Thoreau was a man of letters. *Walden* breathes of the open air, but it was composed in the study. . . . He was a writer whose opportune subject was nature; not a natural scientist.

*   *   *

Thoreau talks about himself, but never about himself alone, always in relation to nature; and he hardly ever wrote a page in which some aspect of it was not recorded as if seen for the first time. He had trained himself to be observant, but his method was not to stare nature in the face but to view it sidelong—receptively. He spoke about 'a true sauntering of the eye,' and it is in ease of manner that he differs from the natural scientist. He tells us facts—the changing conditions of the ice on Walden Pond as spring approaches, the colors of a pickerel's scales, the fragrance of the rare *Azalea nudiflora*—but he invests them with wonder. His transcendentalist contemporaries understood such facts as a language of correspondences. They read nature as though it were a godly kind of Braille, the only difficulties to its comprehension being mechanical. But while Thoreau accepted such a language his interpretation was mystical, not simply moralistic; he wanted 'so to state facts that they shall be significant, shall be myths or mythologic.' The natural world was for him a life to itself, a constant unfolding in whose meaning man himself could share for the sake of fulfillment.

Sherman Paul

. . . Sound was more than the constitutionally preferable vehicle for Thoreau's insights. The other senses were more exacting, in a way—and herein they failed Thoreau—more amenable to scientific use. Sight required attention and could become too particular and limited. Taste and feeling required immediate objects. Smell more nearly approximated the vagueness and unheralded approach of sound, but it did not have an equivalent like silence to make it significant. For sound and silence were Thoreau's grand analogy: silence was a celestial sea of eternity, the general, spiritual and immutable; sound was the particular and momentary bubble on its surface. (*Works*, 1, 418-420) Sound was important to Thoreau for the intimations of silence that it brought him.[1] As distilled from his experience in nature and

An excerpt from "The Wise Silence: Sound as the Agency of Correspondence in Thoreau." From The New England Quarterly, XXII (Dec., 1949), 513, 517-19. Copyright © 1949 by The New England Quarterly. Reprinted by permission of the publisher.

[1] Margaret Fuller expressed the same thought. "The stillness permits me to hear a pure tone from the One in All." *Memoirs*, edited by R. W. Emerson, W. H. Channing, J. F. Clarke (Boston, 1860), II, 83. Herman Melville also identified the in-

society, sound and silence represented for Thoreau what Theodore
Parker called the transient and permanent. Where the other senses
failed him, sound invariably became their surrogate, and put him in
touch with the divine.[2] Sound proclaimed the "soundness," the
spiritual wholeness of the universe. It was this silence, as Thoreau
said, that alone was worthy to be heard. (*Journal*, IV, 472)

#   #   #

. . . The process of attaining a controlled and rewarding union with
nature passed through several stages. There was, of course, that of
fact, which Thoreau found wholly unsatisfactory. The fact, however,
could be transmuted on several levels, as for example in the chapter
"Sounds" in *Walden* (*Works*, II, 123-124). Here the sounds are heard
close at hand and recorded with a rich fusion of detail and meaningful participation. Thoreau begins his passage on the whip-poor-will
"vespers" "scientifically" by stating that it was heard "regularly at
half-past seven." The bird was near enough for him to distinguish
"the cluck after each note. . . ." When he turns to the screech owl,
he is refreshingly literary, perhaps one may say "romantic." Their
wailing is "Jonsonian," a "graveyard ditty, the mutual consolations of
suicide lovers remembering the pangs and the delights of supernal
love in the infernal groves." These sounds were the "regrets and sighs
that would fain be sung," and opened for Thoreau a vista into sad
and melancholy nature. He plays with the sound and his mood and
anthropopathizes: "*Oh-o-o-o-o that I never had been bor-r-r-n!*" The
hooting owl is even more melancholy, a "stereotype" of the "dying
moans of a human being. . . ." It reminds him of "ghouls and idiots
and insane howlings." He tries to imitate it. And later he generalizes
his feelings about owls: they suggest "a vast and undeveloped nature
which men have not recognized. They represent the stark twilight
and unsatisfied thoughts which all have." Only for a moment can
one sense the jumping-off place for further imaginative identifications
similar to Thoreau's spiritual expansion over the call of the wood
thrush. Ending his description of the hooting owl, he writes: "But
now one answers from far woods in a strain made really melodious by
distance . . . and indeed for the most part is suggested only pleasing
associations. . . ."

---

scrutable with silence in *Pierre*, Ch. xiv, "The Journey and the Pamphlet" (New
York, 1929), 284; see also 290, where he berates the Transcendentalists for their assurance that they could get "a Voice out of Silence."

2 Sound, too, was a general way of describing the wholeness of his sensory participation; he used it to represent the activity of all his senses, not merely hearing.
"The sounds which I hear with the consent and coincidence of all my senses, these
are significant and musical; at least, they only are heard." (*Journal*, II, 442).

This is as far as "Sounds" takes one into correspondence. A noisy and bustling chapter, it was appropriately followed by "Solitude." Specific sounds were not especially attractive to Thoreau, but rather the more atmospheric sounds—nature stirred, not nature stirring. At the very beginning of the chapter he describes the state in which his sympathy with nature is best achieved:

> This is a delicious evening, when the whole body is one sense, and im-bibes delight through every pore. I go and come with a strange liberty in Nature, a part of herself. . . . *I see nothing special to attract me, but all the elements unusually congenial to me.* . . . Sympathy with the fluttering alder and poplar leaves almost takes away my breath; yet . . . *my serenity is rippled but not ruffled.* [Italics mine]

Under these conditions "there can be no very black melancholy to him who lives in the midst of nature and has his senses still. There was never yet such a storm but it was Æolian music to a healthy and innocent ear." The raindrops made Thoreau aware of "an infinite and unaccountable friendliness all at once like an atmosphere sus-taining me. . . ." Such solitude was the preferable condition for cor-respondence. It was sympathy with Nature ("Am I not partly leaves and vegetable mould myself?"); it could become transport. And yet— and this was what was so necessary if Thoreau were not to be lost in mysticism—"however intense my experience, I am conscious of the presence and criticism of a part of me, which, as it were, is not a part of me, but a spectator, sharing no experience, but taking note of it, and that is no more I than it is you." Such a high degree of control required a "conscious effort of the mind." It made possible the alternatives Thoreau presented when he wrote: "We are not wholly involved in Nature. I may be either the driftwood in the stream, or Indra in the sky looking down on it." Carried too far in the rôle of control, the intellect turned science-ward; but if intellect were absent there might be an incommunicable ecstasy, and for this Thoreau hungered more and more when the delicate balance between the af-fections (senses) and intellect could no longer be sustained.

*   *   *

. . . Thoreau compacted his most complex moods into the symbol of the telegraph wire. He often referred to it as the Aeolian harp. But Aeolian was not necessarily synonymous with the wire, for Aeo-lian signified any sound produced or borne by the wind. Nature was viewed as a harp at rest, like the soul, passively awaiting the divine inspiration; the vibrating harp produced the Aeolian music, the celestial harmony that Thoreau heard.

Bruce King

. . . *Walden* might be said to illustrate the various kinds of perception found in Emerson's essay [*Nature*]. Thoreau's book, however, is neither an essay, nor philosophy, nor preaching; it is a recreation of the various meanings of nature as experienced by Thoreau. . . . To understand how Thoreau brings out the meanings of nature as experienced by the mind and how such an experience creates moral strength, it is useful to examine the "Ponds" chapter of *Walden*. This, is, I feel, the finest part of the book, and some of the best prose written during the nineteenth century. Thoreau explains that when tired of life in his village he would often "ramble" westward among the local woods and ponds, where he would pick berries for his supper. It is part of Thoreau's seemingly artless method that he introduces his themes in a nonchalant manner. Berries, he says, only yield their true flavor in the countryside, but not to a purchaser or to a farmer who raises them for market:

> It is a vulgar error to suppose that you have tasted huckleberries who never plucked them. A huckleberry never reaches Boston; they have not been known there since they grew on her three hills. The ambrosial and essential part of the fruit is lost with the bloom which is rubbed off in the market cart, and they become mere provender. As long as Eternal Justice reigns, not one innocent huckleberry can be transported thither from the country's hills.

We see here Thoreau's supposedly simple, home-spun, country wit. Of course the pose of a provincial humorist is a literary strategy. Thoreau is introducing a theme he will deal with during the remainder of the chapter: the profit motive despoils the countryside of spiritual "fruits" which cannot be transported into the city. This is an attack on economic progress, and on those who believe that the market-place can sell happiness. It is also an example of Thoreau's artistry. Each image has, like nature, a surface existence and another meaning. If Thoreau's love of nature sometimes seems to derive from a vaguely defined philosophy, there is also a balancing realism that expresses itself in irony. Thoreau explains that he would often stay out at the ponds and go fishing during the night. Sitting in the dark he let his mind be carried away with romantic illusions:

An excerpt from "Thoreau's Walden." *From* Études Anglaises, *XVII (1964), 264-67. Copyright 1964 by* Études Anglaises. *Reprinted by permission of the publisher.*

At length you slowly raise, pulling hand over hand, some horned pout squeaking and squirming to the upper air. It was very queer, especially in dark nights, when your thoughts had wandered to vast and cosmogonal themes in other spheres, to feel this faint jerk, which came to interrupt your dreams and link you to Nature again. It seemed as if I might next cast my line upward into the air, as well as downward into this element, which was scarcely more dense. Thus I caught two fishes as it were with one hook.

Catching the fish brings him back from dreaming to reality. But the fish is also an illustration of his communication with nature.

"The Ponds" slowly builds its meaning through an off-hand manner combining anecdotes and description. There is very little action; scenic descriptions easily take on a multiplicity of meanings. We have been gradually prepared to see a spiritual meaning in Thoreau's description of Walden Pond:

> Walden is blue at one time and green at another, even from the same point of view. Lying between the earth and the heavens, it partakes of the color of both. Viewed from a hilltop it reflects the color of the sky; but near at hand it is of a yellowish tint next the shore where you can see the sand, then a light green, which gradually deepens to a uniform dark green in the body of the pond. In some lights, viewed even from a hilltop, it is of a vivid green next the shore.

There is no false climax in this passage, no feeling of tension, no heavyhandedness in the manipulation of symbols. The description is beautiful in itself; it appears to be a realistic picture of what Thoreau saw. However, if we are sensitive to the fullness of the experience Thoreau conveys, then we may find a deeper meaning. Nature contains both a physical and a spiritual aspect, and Walden Pond reflects both. The perception depends upon the individual's sensitivity.

Thoreau continues to describe the pond and its environment. The water is transparent and clean; it rises and falls at long intervals; some say the pond is bottomless. There is a suggestion that the pond has a fineness and permanence which contrast with the corruptions and impermanence of modern life. Walden Pond is a link to the golden ages: "Successive nations perchance have drank at, admired, and fathomed it, and passed away, and still its water is green and pellucid as ever. . . . Who knows in how many unremembered nations' literatures this has been the Castalian Fountain? or what nymphs presided over it in the Golden Age?"

One reads on in delight not only at the richness with which nature is represented but at the fullness with which Thoreau communicates his experience. We notice the water-fowl on the pond, the swallows skimming overhead, the berries of the shore, and the variety of trees that surround it. Occasionally we stop to muse over the rise and fall of the pond, or the reason why the shore is so regular. There is a still-ness to Thoreau's prose that captures the lack of disturbance in na-ture. Everything seems idyllic:

> It is a soothing employment, on one of those fine days in the fall when all the warmth of the sun is fully appreciated, to sit on a stump on such a height as this, overlooking the pond, and study the dimpling circles which are incessantly inscribed on its otherwise invisible surface amid the reflected skies and trees. Over this great expanse there is no dis-turbance but it is thus at once gently smoothed away and assuaged, as, when a vase of water is jarred, the trembling circles seek the shore and all is smooth again. Not a fish can leap or an insect fall on the pond but it is thus reported in circling dimples, in lines of beauty, as it were the constant welling up of its fountain, the gentle pulsing of its life, the heaving of its breast. The thrills of joy and thrills of pain are indistin-guishable. How peaceful the phenomena of the lake! Again the works of man shine as in the spring. Ay, every leaf and twig and stone and cob-web sparkles now at mid-afternoon as when covered with dew in a spring morning. Every motion of an oar or an insect produces a flash of light; and if an oar falls, how sweet the echo!

Gradually the mood changes. We are reminded that there are fewer waterfowl than in the past. Trees are being cut for profit. The rail-roads now muddy the water with their dirt. During the winters even frozen waters of the lake are cut into blocks for commercial ice. The idyllic life represented by Walden is not a matter of environment, or of retreat from urban life; it is rather a moral question involving the way man chooses to live. We have seen the mercenary benefits of Walden and have seen its forms of beauty. In the description of its waters we can even feel the presence of spiritual forces that link man to his maker. Now we are forced to see Walden as an ideal that will test our moral imagination. It is a prospect of a way of life that de-pends on our spirit and self-discipline. Nature will renew itself despite the ethics of the market-place; the question is whether man can have the courage to find joy in his life once more: "where a forest was cut down last winter another is springing up by its shore as lustily as ever; the same thought is welling up to its surface that was then; it is the same liquid joy and happiness to itself and its Maker, ay, and it *may* be to me."

There are other ponds near Walden and they offer a contrast be-tween the ideal and what life has become. Flint's Pond is larger than

Walden, but it is shallow and not pure. Even the name, Flint's Pond, is significant. It is nature as worshipped under the sign of the dollar, in which woods, beasts, and waters are only seen as resources for production. There is no joy at Flint's Pond. It is not appreciated, or lived with. Its shores are laid bare, and its waterfowl have been chased away. No one bathes in it, looks at it, protects it, or loves it. Thoreau achieves an almost Biblical eloquence in describing the wretched mentality of those who have plundered Flint's Pond. All their qualities are negative. The land has become infertile, stripped of its divinity, and impoverished for future use. No spiritual life remains. The fruits of nature have been picked for economic gain by the farmer,

> who regretted only that it was not English hay or cranberry meadow, —there was nothing to redeem it, forsooth, in his eyes,—and would have drained and sold it for the mud at its bottom. It did not turn his mill, and it was no *privilege* to him to behold it. I respect not his labors, his farm where everything has its price; who would carry the landscape, who would carry his God, to market, if he could get anything for him; who goes to market *for* his god as it is; on whose farm nothing grows free, whose fields bear no crops, whose meadows no flowers, whose trees no fruits, but dollars; who loves not the beauty of his fruits, whose fruits are not ripe for him till they are turned to dollars.

This seems to me to be one of the finest passages in American literature. I cannot read it without thinking of a similar tone in Pound's best invective or a similar vision of the modern commercial wasteland in Eliot's early poems. The chapter concludes with an attack on the American puritan tradition and its belief in the moral superiority of work and profit: "Talk of heaven! ye disgrace earth."

Walden has a structure as seamless as anything in American literature. The book moves forward in increasing spiritual depth and symbolic implications from its initial explanation of how Thoreau left society to study what he could learn from nature, through various stages of spiritual growth, until, at the book's end, a man is reborn, cleansed in spirit. We move from an experience of nature on a basic level of finding sustenance through increasingly deeper forms of perception until we reach what Emerson called "prospects": the realization, symbolized by the "Spring" chapter, that nature offers expanding horizons of possibilities for man's spiritual growth. . . .

Gerry Brenner

In the chapter "Brute Neighbors" from *Walden,* Thoreau creates an animal cosmos that dramatizes his transcendental vision of the divinity of nature with a conciseness found nowhere else in the book. And more important, his cosmos expands in a highly structural pattern. That is, excluding the brief prefatory colloquy between the hermit and the poet, Thoreau displays a highly artistic consciousness in this chapter that invalidates a customary charge of intellectual fragmentation. . . .

On the natural level the animals Thoreau discusses sequentially conform to a paradigmatic sociological world. . . .

After creating this microcosmic world of individual, family, community, and states, Thoreau seems to lose control of his structure; he studies three of the battling ants under the microscope. But instead of disintegrating his world, his minute observations become a metaphor for a necessary stage in understanding the natural world. That is, only by observing nature closely and scientifically, a primary Transcendental dictate, can one see beyond it. An understanding needs not only Thoreau's reverence for the more inherent qualities of animals that seem to epitomize human ideals without human failings, but also an objectivity to see the natural world as fact.

And the subsequent paragraph, a parody of historical documentation of several previous ant wars, also needs to be restored from an easy charge of digression. The humor is necessary for a rounded appreciation of the animal world just as it is necessary for a rounded view of the human. Without the parody, Thoreau's reverence for the animal world could verge on the sententious.

These last two shifts into the masks of scientist and historian provide an artistic pause before . . . [Thoreau progresses] into the second level of the animal cosmos, the unnatural. In contrast with the natural level, which observes the animals instinctively at home in their own environment, this second level focuses upon the "village Bose" (dog) and "domestic cat," aliens from another society. Since they have become "civilized" animals they are no longer naturalized citizens, so to speak, of the animal world. . . .

The alienation of these civilized animals makes for an easy transition from unnatural animals to a preternatural one, the winged cat,

An excerpt from "Thoreau's 'Brute Neighbors': Four Levels of Nature." From Emerson Society Quarterly, *XXXIX (1965), 37-40. Copyright © 1965 by* Emerson Society Quarterly. *Reprinted by permission of the publisher.*

an alien from another world who exceeds what is normal or natural
without being felt as supernatural. . . .

Though the magic of the winged cat is facetious, it provides the
necessary transfer into the section on the loon. Here Thoreau manipu-
lates his discussion to see . . . the very godhead of the animal world.
From the preternatural animal world of the winged cat it is but a
small step to the supernatural world of the loon. And some of
Thoreau's most exciting prose establishes his careful relationship
with and symbolization of the loon. Thoreau dramatizes the divinity
of the loon one afternoon on Walden Pond while trying to outguess
it. Throughout the episode, a metaphor for man's attempt to lay
hold on the mystery of divinity, Thoreau punctuates the quest with
intimations of the loon's powers. Almost at the outset he says that
"the poor bird cannot be omnipresent," a statement that could only
be taken as naive after the bird exhibits such masterful powers of
evasiveness to both the hunters and Thoreau. And the very denial of
the bird's omnipresence flirts at the same time with affirmation. During the actual parrying of moves with the loon, Thoreau time and
again hints at the bird's god-like prowess: its cunning maneuverabil-
ity, its long-windedness and swiftness . . . its unweariableness. . . .
Beyond these physical attributes, Thoreau twice notes his own inability to "divine" the bird's thoughts or whereabouts, the conscious
use of the word "divine" giving another clue to Thoreau's intention.
The bird is further recognized for its ability to accommodate itself
to different environments: ". . . he appeared to know his course as
surely underwater as on the surface and swam much faster there."
Thoreau refers to him once as an "ungainly visitor from another
sphere." The loon's "demoniac laughter," "unearthly howl," superlative "wildest sound" and what Thoreau tongue-in-cheek calls its silli-
ness also suggest the divinity of the mad. Thoreau's conclusion about
the laugh, "that he laughed in derision of my efforts, confident of his
own resources," smacks of a Hardian view of the gods' contemptuous
attitude towards mortals. Finally, in grand prose, Thoreau has the
loon display his divinity by calling in nature to translate him away:

> At length, having come up fifty rods off, he uttered one of those pro-
> longed howls, as if calling on the god of loons to aid him, and immedi-
> ately there came a wind from the east and rippled the surface, and filled
> the whole air with misty rain, and I was impressed as if it were the
> prayer of the loon answered, and his god was angry with me; and so I
> left him disappearing far away on the tumultuous surface.

The value of the episode with the loon is that Thoreau the artist
never gives way to the impulse to be Transcendental apologist, to see
the loon explicitly as only a godhead. His fidelity to the realistic

world is indicated when he confesses that the hunters "were too often successful" in their hunts for the loon. Just as the loon evades Thoreau on the water, Thoreau has it evade an allegorical meaning. The evolution from natural to unnatural to preternatural to supernatural ultimately resists such neat categorization as I have given it since the account of the naturalist is never fully pre-empted by the microcosmic hierarchy that overrides the chapter. Part of the technique to restrain his loon quest from becoming heavy is his mask of naivete, as when he boasts ". . . I was more than a match for him on the surface [of the lake]," or when he assumes that the loon's laugh betrays itself, or, finally, when Thoreau gullibly commends himself by condescending about the bird, "He was indeed a silly loon, I thought."

. . . Yet in spite of his affected smugness . . . his encounter with the loon reasserts, only this time on a metaphysical level, the limitations of man's sight; neither the hunters' "spyglasses" nor Thoreau's naturalist's eye is a match for the loon's omniscience. In accordance with the shift from natural to supernatural noticed earlier, the eye metaphor of the partridge chicks' eyes becomes expanded . . . into Walden Pond itself. That is, the activity on the pond reflects, as do the chicks' eyes, an ideal quality and a divinity which exist in Thoreau's "brute neighbors" and which means much more than is apparent to the casual observer that Thoreau feigns to be. The loon chase reflects his Transcendental vision of the ideal relationship to the animal world, a divine quest that paradoxically achieves understanding through defeat.

Constance Rourke

[In] the lingo of the time Thoreau was "quirky," that is, obstinate and headstrong and full of notions. With all his aversion to distant movement he was not unrelated to the mythical figure of the Yankee peddler; he made the same calculations, many of them close and shrewd, often in the area of bargaining. He had that air of turning the tables on listeners or observers which had long since belonged to the Yankee of the comic mythologies; he used a wry humor in slow prose argument; he kept the habitual composure. Whoever might be his companion Thoreau seemed always alone, like the legendary Yankee. His tough and sinuous reveries were unbroken. "In any

From American Humor *by Constance M. Rourke. Copyright 1931, by Harcourt, Brace & World, Inc.; renewed 1959 by Alice D. Fore. Reprinted by permission of the publishers.*

weather, at any hour of the day or night, I have been anxious to improve the nick of time, and notch it on my stick too; to stand on the meeting of two eternities, the past and the future, which is precisely the present moment; to toe that line." Here was the essence of self-consciousness, revealed in Yankee speech. Yet this always verged toward the abstract, slipping aside from personal revelation, and moving with increasing frequency toward another theme which had engrossed the Yankee, the land. That sense of wild land which had infused the Yankee monologues, creating a spare imagery and metaphor, was pressed by Thoreau back to its source until he obtained a whole subject.

Thoreau greatly deepened the figurative Yankee speech, and soared occasionally into allegory. "I long ago lost a hound, a bay horse, and a turtle-dove, and am still on their trail. Many are the travelers I have spoken to concerning them, describing their tracks and what calls they answered to. I have met one or two who had heard the hound, and the tramp of the horse, and had even seen the dove disappear behind a cloud, and they seemed as anxious to recover them as if they had lost them themselves." This beautiful and cryptic poetry was cast into Thoreau's discourse a little awry: he suddenly stopped, as if unable to pursue further the theme or its implications. It has the partial and fragmentary air which has been seen elsewhere in native fable and figure, rising as from hidden sources, then pausing as though the underlying inspiration were insecure or incomplete.

Frank Davidson

Almost twenty years ago Professor Crawford, in a brief footnote to Thoreau's enigmatic statement in *Walden* about a hound, a bay horse, and a turtle-dove,[1] spoke of its omission from the original manuscript and added the inferences of Van Doren and Raysor as to its meaning.[2] Three years later Edith Peairs called attention to Emerson's having puzzled over the passage, admitting that he did not know its meaning but suggesting that it was a "mythical record of [Thoreau's] disappointments"; H. A. Page conjectured that it perhaps reflected Thoreau's search for the unsophisticated man; F. H. Allen interpreted it as representing "vague desires and aspirations of man's spiritual nature"; and John Burroughs viewed it as a reference to the "fine

"*Thoreau's Hound, Bay Horse, and Turtle-Dove*," by *Frank Davidson. From* The New England Quarterly, *XXVII (1954), 521-24. Copyright © 1954 by* The New England Quarterly. *Reprinted by permission of the publisher.*

[1] *The Writings of Henry David Thoreau* (Boston and New York, 1906), II, 18-19.
[2] *Henry David Thoreau, Representative Selections* (New York, 1934), 359, n. 57.

effluence" of nature.[3] In a further attempt to elucidate the passage Peairs went outside *Walden* for an explanation and, mistakenly perhaps, read into the lines an expression of Thoreau's disillusionment at failing to find an ideal friend. Since *Walden* is an artistically executed unit, the meaning of the three images should, I think, be sought as an integral part of the whole work.

The book has as theme the need of man's awakening to a knowledge of his three possible levels of living—animal, intellectual, and spiritual, instead of merely animal—each with awards for which man will barter life and each with contributions to make to a properly proportioned existence. "The life which men praise and regard as successful," says Thoreau, "is but one kind. Why should we exaggerate any one kind at the expense of others?" [4]

The materials used in the development of this theme the author patterns for order and right emphasis. For example, the story opens with spring and closes with spring, the period of awakening of natural life, of renewal, of purification. Between the beginning and end is a definite structural center, "The Village," a chapter which, by its contrasting account of [the] institutional, materialistic life of the world, emphasizes the theme. "Higher Laws," with its summary and forecast, makes a climax for the story. At proportionate distances from beginning, middle, and end appear the dramatic episodes of the Canadian woodchopper and the Irishman John Field, the former engaged in a contented life at the animal level, unaware of his latencies of intellect and spirit and innocent of the world's perverted sense of values; the latter, too, at the animal level but discontented, troubled by a desire for something better than what he has but addicted to the world's luxuries and lacking faith to make trial of a life that would take him beyond material acquisition. The whole of *Walden* is rhythmical with repetition of the words *spring, dawn, morning, sunrise, awakening, purification*—all connotative of freshness, beginnings, growth, renewal, change. There is not much of disillusionment.

Early in this framework appears the statement about Thoreau's loss long ago of a hound, a bay horse, and a turtle-dove and of his desire to find them. The instinct for them seemed still present. Others, he says, were searching too and deriving some hope from faint sounds and momentary glimpses of these lost possessions. The words *long ago* are significant. They may refer to the author's childhood; preferably they may indicate that stage of civilization where man began to lose his pristine relationship with nature and to assume the conventions of an institutionalized society.

[3] "The Hound, the Bay Horse, and the Turtle-Dove," PMLA, LII, 866-867 (Sept., 1937).
[4] *The Writings*, II, 21.

In suggesting that Thoreau derived his hound-horse-dove combination from Voltaire and that he modified the French expressions for
euphony and rhythm, Peairs may be right,[5] though the words do occur
singly in the text of *Walden*. The hound, in each instance, implies
wildness,[6] as for example in the climactic chapter:

> . . . I found myself ranging the woods, like a half-starved hound, with
> a strange abandonment, seeking some kind of venison which I might
> devour, and no morsel could have been too savage for me. The wildest
> scenes had become unaccountably familiar. I found in myself, and still
> find, an instinct toward a higher, or, as it is named, spiritual life, as do
> most men, and another toward a primitive rank and savage one, and I
> reverence them both. I love the wild not not less than the good.[7]

That the wild should be purified, given its proper place, but not
refined away Thoreau illustrates with a boy's being allowed to go to
the woods with a gun. With proper development the boy, grown to
manhood, will continue his visits to the woods but, after a time, without the gun.

The horse is introduced incidentally but somewhat significantly in
the account of the winged cat that was sometimes seen in the region
near the pond.

> This would have been the right kind of cat for me to keep [says Thoreau],
> if I had kept any; for why should not a poet's cat be winged as well as
> his horse? [8]

The attaching of the adjective *bay* to this Pegasus may have derived from Thoreau's remembrance of Gulliver's observation on the
Houyhnhnms, that "the white, the sorrel, and the iron-gray, were not
so exactly shaped as the bay, the dapple-gray, and the black. . . ." [9]
In fact, the whole concept of the bay horse may be a mingling of
classical myth and Swiftian fantasy, for the word *Houyhnhnm*, said
Gulliver, signified "a *horse*, and in its etymology, *the perfection of
nature*." [10] The horse, then, becomes a symbol of the poetic life—of
intellectual creativity.

[5] PMLA, LII, 863-869.
[6] *The Writings*, II, 232, 247, 305, 307-308.
[7] *The Writings*, II, 232. Thoreau had spoken spiritedly of this wildness in *A Week
on the Concord and Merrimack Rivers* (Boston, 1929), 54-55: "There is in my nature . . . a single yearning toward all wildness. . . . Gardening is civil and social,
but it wants the vigor and freedom of the forest and the outlaw. There may be an
excess of cultivation as well as of anything else, until civilization becomes pathetic."
[8] *The Writings*, II, 258.
[9] Jonathan Swift, *Gulliver's Travels* (New York, 1920), 262.
[10] *Gulliver's Travels*, 239.

The dove is mentioned twice in *Walden* in addition to the reference in the passage under discussion; once it is associated with a saint:

> It would be well, perhaps, if we were to spend more of our days and nights without any obstruction between us and the celestial bodies, if the poet did not speak so much from under a roof, or the saint dwell there so long. Birds do not sing in caves, nor do doves cherish their innocence in dovecots.[11]

One may be sure that Thoreau knew of the Hebrew law mentioned by St. Luke prescribing the sacrifice of doves in the rite of purification.

The hound, the bay horse, and the turtle-dove seem to be respectively for Thoreau symbols of a wildness that keeps man in touch with nature, intellectual stimulus, and purification of spirit. In combination they characterize man in his true state. But they are constantly in danger of being obscured or lost through man's inertia, through his living at a material level only, through his institutionalized life.

William Bysshe Stein

Thoreau's familiar digression on the hound, bay horse, and turtle-dove in Chapter I of *Walden* has to be associated with the preliminary statement which the sequence of images illustrates: "You will pardon some obscurities, for there are more secrets in my trade than in most men's, and yet not involuntarily kept, but inseparable from its very nature." Since, as we learn a moment later, this trade "is with the Celestial Empire," it seems to follow that his quest for these lost creatures is directly related to his search for divine wisdom. But inasmuch as such an experience involves transformation, not merely information, it cannot be communicated verbally. Like his sojourn on Walden Pond, its meaning has to be inferred from the way of life which is adumbrated, what he calls in the complemental verses to Chapter I "that heroic virtue/For which antiquity hath left no name,/But patterns only, such as Hercules."

As Tom Peete Cross's *Motif-Index of Early Irish Literature* (Bloomington, 1952) clearly proves, the pattern in question, with innumerable variations, is frequently encountered in the myth and folklore of Ire-

11 *The Writings*, II, 31.

"*Thoreau's Hound, Bay Horse, and Turtledove*," by *William Bysshe Stein*. From The Thoreau Society Bulletin, *LXVII (1959), 1. Copyright* © *1959 by* The Thoreau Society Bulletin. *Reprinted by permission of the publisher.*

land. More often than not, it is connected with a test and/or quest whose successful completion depends upon the aid of a supernatural horse, dog, or bird. I would like to suggest that Thoreau heard such a story in his, no doubt, numerous conversations with the Irish immigrants who worked on the railroad adjacent to the pond. And it was probably a version of "The Story of Conn-eda; or the Golden Apples of Lough Erne," a work which is included in William Butler Yeats' *Irish Fairy and Folk Tales* (Modern Library; New York, n.d.).

This tale involves a youthful hero who is sent on a dangerous quest into the land of fairy for three golden apples, a steed, and a hound, all possessing magical powers. This test, devised by a wicked stepmother who seeks to deprive him of his rightful kingship of Ireland, appears to promise certain death. However, a puissant druid advises him to trust his luck to a nondescript horse which guides him to the elusive Bird of the Human Head, from whom he receives all the help needed to fulfill his mission. But not until he undergoes the most arduous physical and moral ordeals does he procure the three extraordinary trophies and, in the process, supreme wisdom. In short, he re-enacts a pattern of heroic virtue that qualifies him to reign in the place of a faultless father. Symbolically, of course, Thoreau emulates the accomplishment of Conn-eda, for he too perfects his life by trusting his instincts (the animal in man) to lead him to his goal of self-understanding. This inadequate paraphrase, I must confess, hardly does justice to the astounding imaginative richness of the folktale, for its implications are keyed to the shape-shifting rhythms of *Walden* itself.

I might add that the adventures of Conn-eda are paralleled to a considerable extent in another Irish myth, "The King of Ireland and the Queen of Lonesome Island." Once again it is an unimpressive horse that insures the hero's successful quest. Strikingly enough, this story, like the one above, still floated in the oral traditions of Ireland in the latter part of the nineteenth-century; see Jeremiah Curtin's *Myths and Folk-lore of Ireland* (Boston, 1906).

A Slight Sound at Evening

by E. B. White

(Allen Cove, Summer, 1954)

In his journal for July 10-12, 1841, Thoreau wrote: "A slight sound at evening lifts me up by the ears, and makes life seem inexpressibly serene and grand. It may be in Uranus, or it may be in the shutter." The book into which he later managed to pack both Uranus and the shutter was published in 1854, and now, a hundred years having gone by, "Walden," its serenity and grandeur unimpaired, still lifts us up by the ears, still translates for us that language we are in danger of forgetting, "which all things and events speak without metaphor, which alone is copious and standard."

"Walden" is an oddity in American letters. It may very well be the oddest of our distinguished oddities. For many it is a great deal too odd, and for many it is a particular bore. I have not found it to be a well-liked book among my acquaintances, although usually spoken of with respect, and one literary critic for whom I have the highest regard can find no reason why anyone gives "Walden" a second thought. To admire the book is, in fact, something of an embarrassment, for the mass of men have an indistinct notion that its author was a sort of Nature Boy.

I think it is of some advantage to encounter the book at a period in one's life when the normal anxieties and enthusiasms and rebellions of youth closely resemble those of Thoreau in that spring of 1845 when he borrowed an axe, went out to the woods, and began to whack down some trees for timber. Received at such a juncture, the book is like an invitation to life's dance, assuring the troubled recipient that no matter what befalls him in the way of success or failure he will always be welcome at the party—that the music is played for

him, too, if he will but listen and move his feet. In effect, that is what
the book is—an invitation, unengraved; and it stirs one as a young
girl is stirred by her first big party bid. Many think it a sermon; many
set it down as an attempt to rearrange society; some think it an exercise in nature-loving; some find it a rather irritating collection of in-
spirational puffballs by an eccentric show-off. I think it none of these.
It still seems to me the best youth's companion yet written by an
American, for it carries a solemn warning against the loss of one's
valuables, it advances a good argument for traveling light and trying
new adventures, it rings with the power of positive adoration, it contains religious feeling without religious images, and it steadfastly refuses to record bad news. Even its pantheistic note is so pure as to be
noncorrupting—pure as the flute-note blown across the pond on those
faraway summer nights. If our colleges and universities were alert,
they would present a cheap pocket edition of the book to every senior
upon graduating, along with his sheepskin, or instead of it. Even if
some senior were to take it literally and start felling trees, there could
be worse mishaps: the axe is older than the Dictaphone and it is just
as well for a young man to see what kind of chips he leaves before
listening to the sound of his own voice. And even if some were to get
no farther than the table of contents, they would learn how to name
eighteen chapters by the use of only thirty-nine words and would see
how sweet are the uses of brevity.

If Thoreau had merely left us an account of a man's life in the
woods, or if he had simply retreated to the woods and there recorded
his complaints about society, or even if he had contrived to include
both records in one essay, "Walden" would probably not have lived
a hundred years. As things turned out, Thoreau, very likely without
knowing quite what he was up to, took man's relation to nature and
man's dilemma in society and man's capacity for elevating his spirit
and he beat all these matters together, in a wild free interval of self-
justification and delight, and produced an original omelette from
which people can draw nourishment in a hungry day. "Walden" is
one of the first of the vitamin-enriched American dishes. If it were a
little less good than it is, or even a little less queer, it would be an
abominable book. Even as it is, it will continue to baffle and annoy
the literal mind and all those who are unable to stomach its caprices
and imbibe its theme. Certainly the plodding economist will continue to have rough going if he hopes to emerge from the book with
a clear system of economic thought. Thoreau's assault on the Concord society of the mid-nineteenth century has the quality of a modern Western: he rides into the subject at top speed, shooting in all
directions. Many of his shots ricochet and nick him on the rebound,
and throughout the melee there is a horrendous cloud of incon-

sistencies and contradictions, and when the shooting dies down and the air clears, one is impressed chiefly by the courage of the rider and by how splendid it was that somebody should have ridden in there and raised all that ruckus.

When he went to the pond, Thoreau struck an attitude and did so deliberately, but his posturing was not to draw the attention of others to him but rather to draw his own attention more closely to himself. "I learned this at least by my experiment: that if one advances confidently in the direction of his dreams, and endeavors to live the life which he has imagined, he will meet with a success unexpected in common hours." The sentence has the power to resuscitate the youth drowning in his sea of doubt. I recall my exhilaration upon reading it, many years ago, in a time of hesitation and despair. It restored me to health. And now in 1954 when I salute Henry Thoreau on the hundredth birthday of his book, I am merely paying off an old score—or an installment on it.

In his journal for May 3-4, 1838—Boston to Portland—he wrote: "Midnight—head over the boat's side—between sleeping and waking— with glimpses of one or more lights in the vicinity of Cape Ann. Bright moonlight—the effect heightened by seasickness." The entry illuminates the man, as the moon the sea on that night in May. In Thoreau the natural scene was heightened, not depressed, by a disturbance of the stomach, and nausea met its match at last. There was a steadiness in at least one passenger if there was none in the boat. Such steadiness (which in some would be called intoxication) is at the heart of "Walden"—confidence, faith, the discipline of looking always at what is to be seen, undeviating gratitude for the life-everlasting that he found growing in his front yard. "There is nowhere recorded a simple and irrepressible satisfaction with the gift of life, any memorable praise of God." He worked to correct that deficiency. "Walden" is his acknowledgment of the gift of life. It is the testament of a man in a high state of indignation because (it seemed to him) so few ears heard the uninterrupted poem of creation, the morning wind that forever blows. If the man sometimes wrote as though all his readers were male, unmarried, and well-connected, it is because he gave his testimony during the callow years, and, for that matter, never really grew up. To reject the book because of the immaturity of the author and the bugs in the logic is to throw away a bottle of good wine because it contains bits of the cork.

Thoreau said he required of every writer, first and last, a simple and sincere account of his own life. Having delivered himself of this chesty dictum, he proceeded to ignore it. In his books and even in his enormous journal, he withheld or disguised most of the facts from which an understanding of his life could be drawn. "Walden," sub-

titled "Life in the Woods," is not a simple and sincere account of a
man's life, either in or out of the woods; it is an account of a man's
journey into the mind, a toot on the trumpet to alert the neighbors.
Thoreau was well aware that no one can alert his neighbors who is
not wide awake himself, and he went to the woods (among other
reasons) to make sure that he would stay awake during his broadcast.
What actually took place during the years 1845-47 is largely unre-
corded, and the reader is excluded from the private life of the author,
who supplies almost no gossip about himself, a great deal about his
neighbors and about the universe.

As for me, I cannot in this short ramble give a simple and sincere
account of my own life, but I think Thoreau might find it instructive
to know that this memorial essay is being written in a house that,
through no intent on my part, is the same size and shape as his own
domicile on the pond—about ten by fifteen, tight, plainly finished,
and at a little distance from my Concord. The house in which I sit
this morning was built to accommodate a boat, not a man, but by
long experience I have learned that in most respects it shelters me
better than the larger dwelling where my bed is, and which, by
design, is a manhouse not a boathouse. Here in the boathouse I am a
wilder and, it would appear, a healthier man, by a safe margin. I have
a chair, a bench, a table, and I can walk into the water if I tire of
the land. My house fronts a cove. Two fishermen have just arrived to
spot fish from the air—an osprey and a man in a small yellow plane
who works for the fish company. The man, I have noticed, is less well
equipped than the hawk, who can dive directly on his fish and carry
it away, without telephoning. A mouse and a squirrel share the house
with me. The building is, in fact, a multiple dwelling, a semidetached
affair. It is because I am semidetached while here that I find it
possible to transact this private business with the fewest obstacles.

There is also a woodchuck here, living forty feet away under the
wharf. When the wind is right, he can smell my house; and when the
wind is contrary, I can smell his. We both use the wharf for sunning,
taking turns, each adjusting his schedule to the other's convenience.
Thoreau once ate a woodchuck. I think he felt he owed it to his
readers, and that it was little enough, considering the indignities they
were suffering at his hands and the dressing-down they were taking.
(Parts of "Walden" are pure scold.) Or perhaps he ate the woodchuck
because he believed every man should acquire strict business habits,
and the woodchuck was destroying his market beans. I do not know.
Thoreau had a strong experimental streak in him. It is probably no
harder to eat a woodchuck than to construct a sentence that lasts a
hundred years. At any rate, Thoreau is the only writer I know who

prepared himself for his great ordeal by eating a woodchuck; also the only one who got a hangover from drinking too much water. (He was drunk the whole time, though he seldom touched wine or coffee or tea.)

Here in this compact house where I would spend one day as deliberately as Nature if I were not being pressed by THE YALE REVIEW, and with a woodchuck (as yet uneaten) for neighbor, I can feel the companionship of the occupant of the pondside cabin in Walden woods, a mile from the village, near the Fitchburg right of way. Even my immediate business is no barrier between us: Thoreau occasionally batted out a magazine piece, but was always suspicious of any sort of purposeful work that cut into his time. A man, he said, should take care not to be thrown off the track by every nutshell and mosquito's wing that falls on the rails.

There has been much guessing as to why he went to the pond. To set it down to escapism is, of course, to misconstrue what happened. Henry went forth to battle when he took to the woods, and "Walden" is the report of a man torn by two powerful and opposing drives—the desire to enjoy the world (and not be derailed by a mosquito wing) and the urge to set the world straight. One cannot join these two successfully, but sometimes, in rare cases, something good or even great results from the attempt of the tormented spirit to reconcile them. Henry went forth to battle, and if he set the stage himself, if he fought on his own terms and with his own weapons, it was because it was his nature to do things differently from most men, and to act in a cocky fashion. If the pond and the woods seemed a more plausible site for a house than an in-town location, it was because a cowbell made for him a sweeter sound than a churchbell. "Walden," the book, makes the sound of a cowbell, more than a churchbell, and proves the point, although both sounds are in it, and both remarkably clear and sweet. He simply preferred his churchbell at a little distance.

I think one reason he went to the woods was a perfectly simple and commonplace one—and apparently he thought so, too. "At a certain season of our life," he wrote, "we are accustomed to consider every spot as the possible site of a house." There spoke the young man, a few years out of college, who had not yet broken away from home. He hadn't married, and he had found no job that measured up to his rigid standards of employment, and like any young man, or young animal, he felt uneasy and on the defensive until he had fixed himself a den. Most young men, of course, casting about for a site, are content merely to draw apart from their kinfolks. Thoreau, convinced that the greater part of what his neighbors called good was bad, withdrew from a great deal more than family: he pulled out of everything for a while, to serve everybody right for being so stuffy, and to try his own prejudices on the dog.

The house-hunting sentence above, which starts the Chapter called "Where I Lived, and What I Lived For," is followed by another passage that is worth quoting here because it so beautifully illustrates the offbeat prose that Thoreau was master of, a prose at once strictly disciplined and wildly abandoned. "I have surveyed the country on every side within a dozen miles of where I live," continued this delirious young man. "In imagination I have bought all the farms in succession, for all were to be bought, and I knew their price. I walked over each farmer's premises, tasted his wild apples, discoursed on husbandry with him, took his farm at his price, at any price, mortgaging it to him in my mind; even put a higher price on it—took everything but a deed of it—took his word for his deed, for I dearly love to talk—cultivated it, and him to some extent, I trust, and withdrew when I had enjoyed it long enough, leaving him to carry it on." A copydesk man would get a double hernia trying to clean up that sentence for the management, but the sentence needs no fixing, for it perfectly captures the meaning of the writer and the quality of the ramble.

"Wherever I sat, there I might live, and the landscape radiated from me accordingly." Thoreau, the home-seeker, sitting on his hummock with the entire State of Massachusetts radiating from him, is to me the most humorous of the New England figures, and "Walden" the most humorous of the books, though its humor is almost continuously subsurface and there is nothing funny anywhere, except a few weak jokes and bad puns that rise to the surface like the perch in the pond that rose to the sound of the maestro's flute. Thoreau tended to write in sentences, a feat not every writer is capable of, and "Walden" is, rhetorically speaking, a collection of certified sentences, some of them, it would now appear, as indestructible as they are errant. The book is distilled from the vast journals, and this accounts for its intensity: he picked out bright particles that pleased his eye, whirled them in the kaleidoscope of his content, and produced the pattern that has endured—the color, the form, the light.

On this its hundredth birthday, Thoreau's "Walden" is pertinent and timely. In our uneasy season, when all men unconsciously seek a retreat from a world that has got almost completely out of hand, his house in the Concord woods is a haven. In our culture of gadgetry and the multiplicity of convenience, his cry "Simplicity, simplicity, simplicity!" has the insistence of a fire alarm. In the brooding atmosphere of war and the gathering radioactive storm, the innocence and serenity of his summer afternoons are enough to burst the remembering heart, and one gazes back upon that pleasing interlude—its confidence, its purity, its deliberateness—with awe and wonder, as one would look upon the face of a child asleep.

"This small lake was of most value as a neighbor in the intervals of a gentle rain-storm in August, when, both air and water being perfectly still, but the sky overcast, midafternoon had all the serenity of evening, and the wood-thrush sang around, and was heard from shore to shore." Now, in the perpetual overcast in which our days are spent, we hear with extra perception and deep gratitude that song, tying century to century. . . .

The Intellectual Heritage of Thoreau

by Norman Foerster

"Every man," says Emerson, "is a bundle of his ancestors." Of Thoreau's ancestors, there is good reason to believe that the most significant were not his parents, and their parents, but rather certain ideas and moral traits in the midst of which, as a boy and young man, he lived and moved and had his being,—drawing them in with the very air that he breathed, building them, unconsciously, into the personality known as Henry David Thoreau.

Born in 1817, he was fifteen years younger than Emerson; that is one of the cardinal facts in his biography, a kind of major premise never to be lost sight of in a study of his inner life. He had not yet graduated from Harvard College when Emerson's *Nature* was published. In other words, instead of being a precursor or an inaugurator of New England Transcendentalism, he was in a sense a product of that movement—a child and not a parent. In 1825, when Thoreau was only eight years old, Emerson went to his quiet retreat in Divinity Hall to prepare himself for the ministry—to study, that is, for Thoreau, as well as for himself. The long, hard way from orthodoxy to an emancipated devotion to the moral sentiment Emerson may be said to have traveled for his young friend, who reached the goal without being obliged to fight his way to it. Thoreau was never ordained, never endured periods of keen questioning (though, as he says, faith ever keeps doubts in her pay), never went to the New Hampshire hills for a spiritual struggle, never resigned a pastorate, never was the occasion of widespread scandal; all this he experienced, in the main, vicariously, almost without a pang. He was not denied the advantage of the experience; he received the benefit without the labor— he inherited Trancendentalism.

This is hardly the place for a fresh attempt to discover the hidden springs of that elusive movement and to trace the course of the several tributaries to the main stream; so much has been done often enough, if never quite satisfactorily. Still, we cannot afford to proceed

"The Intellectual Heritage of Thoreau," by Norman Foerster. From The Texas Review, *II (1916-17), 192-212. Copyright © by* The Texas Review. *Reprinted by permission of the author and publisher.*

without a word, however allusive, regarding the origins of the movement.

New England Transcendentalism grew out of Unitarianism, which in turn had grown out of Calvinism. These three modes of interpreting the ways of God to man differed as much in spirit as in doctrine. The positive Puritan mind dwelt much on such dogmas as total depravity and eternal punishment; the critical Unitarian mind affected what Emerson aptly characterized as "the pale negations of Boston Unitarianism"; and the emancipated mind of Transcendentalism, passionately aware of the shortcomings of Puritan and Unitarian alike, yet owing much to both, was more and more inclined to believe that each of us makes his own world of beauty, truth, and goodness. For both spirit and doctrine, New England Transcendentalism was largely indebted to Europe: Rousseau, the French Revolution, Kant and his successors in German philosophy, the Romantic Movement in Germany and in England,—these instigated the American Romantic Movement and in large degree supplied both substance and point of view. New England, however, despite a century of prose and reason, was still at bottom Puritan New England, and we may therefore say that Puritanism contributed much that was characteristic of the period. Finally, the literary interests of New England being greatly extended by the new spirit, various literatures were drawn upon almost for the first time (the literature of the Orient, for instance), and the Classics were read—one can hardly say "studied" of a Transcendentalist—with something of the zeal of that earlier and more exuberant Renaissance of fourteenth century Italy.

The movement resulting from these influences was so complex that perhaps no one, from that day to this, has felt that he fully understood it. To state what Transcendentalism was is indeed a hazardous undertaking, since the faithful members of the sect apparently agreed only in disagreeing.[1] Yet, underlying all the protean vagaries of mind and mood, there was a fairly definite common philosophy, or point of view, which was the creed of the Transcendentalists and which they applied to the various departments of life, not least to social life and manners. Emerson has described this philosophy, or point of view.[2] Defining Transcendentalism in a single word as Idealism, he draws a contrast between "the skeptical philosophy of Locke, which insisted that there was nothing in the intellect which was not previously in the experience of the senses," and the intuitive philosophy of Kant, which demonstrated the existence of certain ways of per-

---

[1] They called themselves "the club of the like-minded; I suppose because no two of us thought alike." (James Freeman Clarke, quoted in Cabot's life of Emerson, 1, 249.)

[2] "The Transcendentalist," in *Nature. Addresses and Lectures.*

ception, or Transcendental forms, "which did not come by experience, but through which experience was acquired." Enlarging freely Kant's conception, the Transcendentalists applied the term *Transcendental* to "whatever belongs to the class of intuitive thought," to whatever, that is, *transcends* the ordinary experience of the senses. The mind operating in the sphere of the experience of the senses is the Understanding; the mind operating in the sphere of the intuitive is the Reason. The possibility of transcending the ordinary experience of the senses is constant—since the divine is immanent in the world, and the soul of the individual has access to the soul of the whole, or Oversoul, as Emerson called it. From this intoxicating conception results the idea of practical individualism, or Self-reliance. Intuition, self-reliance, following one's genius, these are the central words in the thoughts of the Transcendentalists.

Inadequate as this summary of necessity is, it will serve as a reminder of many of the facts of New England Transcendentalism that, through oral tradition and through the writing of numberless books, have become common knowledge. The America of that time is not the America of today, even though Emerson, the chief of the band of idealists, has been dead not much more than three decades, and Mr. Frank B. Sanborn, "the last of the Transcendentalists," is still living a useful life in Concord; but just because that day does seem remote, we have acquired perspective, if not insight, and can readily conjure up a picture of the life of that period—of the saintly and oracular Emerson, leaving his company of idealists in the library in order to confer with the woodman, confessing, "We must attend to these things as if they were real"; of the odd poet-naturalist at Walden, sunning himself and dreaming undescribed dreams, or taking the temperature of his beloved Musketaquid; of Bronson Alcott, latter-day Plato and Pythagoras, starving family and friends at Fruitlands in the quest of a spiritual mode of life; of Margaret Fuller, self-appointed Goethe in petticoats,—"rich in friends, rich in experience, rich in culture,"—holding her attenuated conversations on Greek mythology at twenty dollars for ten sessions. It is a charming dream-world to us of the Twentieth Century, the century of the World-war—pretty and ideal, like the world of the pastoral—and serves to refresh weary minds and weary souls. But to conceive it only thus is to misconceive it, for to those who lived in it, it was intensely real,—a time when the drowse of tradition suddenly snapt and real life began, a time when horizons lifted and drew back and spread new visions to the view of enraptured men, a time when the infinite seemed about to incorporate itself in the finite as never before, a time of reform as well as of self-culture, when men leaned on their souls as did the

Puritans of old, and passionately strove to make reason and the will of God prevail.

It was in this environment, in its earlier aspect, that Thoreau found himself in his formative period. A sensitive nature in the receptive years could not but respond to the energy and aspiration everywhere surging round it; and, indeed, Thoreau may be said to have utilized everything in his environment. To nothing that was typical of Transcendentalism was he indifferent—he opposed what he did not espouse. Despite his inferiority to Emerson in certain respects—and those perhaps the highest—he was the Transcendental type at its purest; for the greatness of Emerson is in the main universal—he transcended Transcendentalism—whereas Thoreau is of Transcendentalism all compact.

To determine with some precision what Thoreau derived from the movement, to ascertain what in general his spiritual and intellectual heritage was, we have only to go to his writings, and there to seek answer to the questions: Who were the great minds, or the lesser minds, that he knew well enough to discuss? and what was it that he owed to those to whom he was largely indebted? It has too often been repeated, on the flimsiest authority, that Thoreau was a kind of understudy of Emerson, that he was indebted to Emerson for everything from ideas to voice and carriage of the head. This assertion has been attacked by Thoreau's champions with more zeal than evidence; but one need only glance at his early writings, such as the *Week on the Concord and Merrimac* (that "mine of quotations from good authors") and the first volume of the *Journal* (covering the formative years 20-30 in his life), to be convinced that his indebtedness to Emerson, however obvious it may be, can hardly be accepted in so offhand a manner, and even a critical reading of all his works, with special attention to these early writings, leaves one in some doubt as to what the primary influences on his work really were. Despite the ample material, one cannot be certain that Thoreau really discloses his sympathies and antipathies and indifferences, since failure to mention a writer, even in twenty volumes, does not indicate conclusively that the writer repels or bores, any more than frequent mention indicates conclusively that the writer attracts. But although one can hardly draw such inferences too carefully, most of them are fairly certain to be trustworthy.

Thoreau's poet friend, Ellery Channing, in his amorphous biography, wrote a pleasant chapter on Thoreau's reading, which contains a good deal of authentic information. He tells us, for instance, this: "His reading was done with a pen in his hand: he made what he called 'Fact-books,'—citations which concerned his studies." Thoreau reading with pen in hand is almost a scholarly picture; the luxurious modern reader, reclining on a bed of brown needles under a pine tree, in this day of out-of-doors reading, misconceives Thoreau if he imagines himself to be imitating him. Again: "A good and sufficient academic and college training had made him a Latin and Greek scholar, with good knowledge of French, and some acquaintance with Italian, Spanish, and German"; obviously, there was no need—whatever the fact—of his receiving his learning at second-hand, through Emerson. And again: "He had no favorites among the French and Germans and I do not recall a modern writer except Carlyle and Ruskin whom he valued much." Here we may profitably pause.

It is perfectly obvious that no French writers meant much to Thoreau; with regard to German writers the fact is not quite so clear. German philosophy was unquestionably outside the range of his interest, but what of Goethe? Thoreau himself confessed that he was "not much acquainted with the works of Goethe." On the other hand, he advised a correspondent to read Goethe's Autobiography "by all means," contrasted Carlyle's style with the lasting style of Goethe, and commented with approval on his air of truth. On the whole it is clear that by the time Carlyle's fervid worship, becoming Emerson's dutiful study, had passed to Thoreau, it had lost all its heat. Doubtless Thoreau, like Emerson, could not accept moral laxity in "such as *he*," though I find no trace of this objection; in the *Week* his main objection apparently is that Goethe is too well-bred—lacks the savage element, the primitive virtues.

In his reading in English literature of the eighteenth and nineteenth centuries, the outstanding names are Wordsworth, Coleridge, and Carlyle. In spite of the fact that Channing coupled Ruskin with Carlyle, it seems certain, on *a priori* grounds, that Ruskin was not Thoreau's man; and besides, Thoreau actually mentioned him rarely, and then always in a carping or disappointed mood. Coleridge, again, was less important to him than Carlyle. As for Wordsworth, the favorite poet of the Transcendentalists, I am inclined to think that Thoreau owed far more to him than has yet been recognized.

Aside from the resemblances between the two in their view of nature, the persistency of Thoreau's allusions to Wordsworth is significant: "I have been too much with the world, as the poet might say"; "Heaven lies about us, as in our infancy"—when music is heard; he is "reminded," in a moment of sudden receptivity, "of the way in which Wordsworth so coldly speaks of some natural scenes or visions 'giving him pleasure' "; " 'For life is a forgetting,' etc."—surely such remarks betoken a familiar acquaintance with "the poet." Wordsworth he praises for his distinct vision, his simple truth and beauty, his simple Homeric health (which Carlyle lacks), his "unquestionable and persevering genius," his "simple, epic country life in these days of confusion and turmoil." On the other side, he declares that Wordsworth has "less simple pathos and feminine gentleness than Chaucer"; in another mood, when gentleness was not at a premium, he "is too tame for the Chippeway—we want the Indian's report of Nature." What he owed to Wordsworth coincided, in general, with what he praised him for,—his sincerity, and health, and simplicity, perhaps the example of his country life; but to this we should add nearly the whole of Wordsworth's feelings for nature, which is reflected, in one way or another, throughout Thoreau's writings,—nature as a teacher, the idea of impassioned recollection, the idea of "wise passiveness," and so on. To be sure, Thoreau's attitude toward nature would no doubt have been very much what it was even if he had never read a line of Wordsworth's poetry; but we may at least assume that Wordsworth accentuated certain of his attitudes and moods. Such passages as the following suggest a fundamental influence: "Once I was part and parcel of Nature; now I am observant of her." "*Mem.* Wordsworth's observations on relaxed attention." A transient acquaintance with any phenomenon is not enough, he writes, "you must *remember* it and be reminded of it long afterward, while it lies remotely fair and elysian." "I must receive my life as passively as the willow leaf that flutters over the brook. . . . I will wait the breezes patiently, and grow as Nature shall determine." If these be not echoes but original sound, they ring the more resolutely because another had uttered them before. If Wordsworth did not instil in Thoreau the germs of new thought and feeling, he unquestionably is important as a reinforcing influence.

In the case of the remaining recent English writer, Carlyle, the influence is still harder to determine. The difficulty is, of course, to ascertain what came to Thoreau directly, and what through Emerson, one of Carlyle's earliest admirers and truest friends. Fortunately, virtually all of his writing on Carlyle occurs in one place,—his article on *Thomas Carlyle and His Works,* which he wrote in the first Walden year, and for which he had prepared himself, by reading and taking notes, in the formative years 20-30. This article, a candid and able piece of critical writing, indicates with some definiteness the nature of Carlyle's influence on him. How large an influence he was is expressed concisely in this sentence: "He has been England to us," and in this: "His writings are a gospel to the young of this generation." How penetrating an influence, is suggested by this: "merely reading . . . is not enough: you must almost have written these books yourself. Only he who [like Thoreau] has had the good fortune to read them in the nick of time, in the most perceptive and recipient season of life [20-30], can give any adequate account of them [such as the present article on Thomas Carlyle and his works]." Yet this article fails to single out the great ideas that Carlyle extolled so passionately. Much is said, and said aptly, of Carlyle's moods, but hardly anything of his matter. Is it likely that Carlyle's ideas were of little moment to Thoreau? Oddly enough, that is doubtless the case. For Carlyle's themes, Thoreau cared little enough, for his ideas little more, at least in the form which Carlyle gave them; but for his style he cared a great deal. "The style," he says, "is worth attending to, as one of the most important features of the man which we at this distance can discern." He attends to it liberally, discussing it directly in almost a fifth of the essay and indirectly in most of the rest. On the whole, his discussion is about as satisfactory a criticism of Carlyle's style as has yet been written. He had studied Carlyle with an alert mind, that is clear,—he even ventures the remark, as Froude does later, that Carlyle never wrote a single obscure line, or half line, and presently bestows on him the ineffable compliment of likening his style to a New England landscape. "He has a style," he says elsewhere in the essay, "which can be imitated"; and this we may take, I think, as unconscious confession. The style of the whole essay suggests Carlyle. A single sentence will illustrate:

> How, after all, he gets his living; what proportion of his daily bread he earns by day-labour or job-work with his pen, what he inherits, what steals,—questions whose answers are so significant, and not to be omitted in his biography,—we, alas! are unable to answer here.

That somewhat choppy period is surely Carlylean. The abundance of punctuation in this article indicates, if nothing else does, imitation of Carlyle. I have amused myself by counting the number of punctuation marks per page in this essay and in some of Thoreau's more typical writing (examining in all perhaps six or eight pages); in the article on Carlyle the number is usually larger by a fourth. How much Thoreau's work as a whole owes to Carlyle's style is hard to say. In one of his *Journals* he wrote in the margin "Carlyleish." Though little of his work suggests Carlyle,—for after all his style is preponderantly his own,—yet, as in the case of Wordsworth's influence, we may safely assume, I think, that Carlyle intensified tendencies latent in Thoreau, made his pointed, concrete style more pointed, more concrete, and added something to the occasional grimness of his humor. So far as direct influence is concerned, doubtless Carlyle's style is most important. His "gospel" reached him, one suspects, very largely through random suggestions from Emerson in their walks and talks at Concord.

There seems to be good reason for believing that, in general, what Thoreau received from Emerson he found in the man himself, rather than in his books. The whole question of Thoreau's relation to Emerson is too complicated for discussion in this paper. At least, however, we may safely say this: that, from the man and his books, especially the former, Thoreau received a great deal, including "philosophy" and literary interests. The wavering outlines of his philosophy tend to coincide with the wavering outlines of Emerson's. Roughly, the same may be said of his literary interests. Those heroes or representative men who, in the flesh, were Europe itself to Emerson, he and Thoreau had doubtless discussed many a time, in the allusive Transcendental manner. His interest in Goethe, such as it was, very likely came from Emerson; and Emerson must have fortified, if he did not instil, a love of the older English poets, of the Classics, and of the Oriental religious books.

In an interesting passage in the *Week* Thoreau remarks that to an American reader, "the comparatively recent literature of Europe often appears partial and clannish; and notwithstanding the limited range of his own sympathies and studies, the European writer who presumes that he is speaking for the world is perceived by him to speak only for that corner of it which he inhabits." A hasty reader will conclude that this is provincialism scenting provincialism, but it is not. For one thing, is it not true? Is not Goethe alone to be exempted from the charge of partiality and clannishness, and not all of him? It is highly creditable to Thoreau that, despite his own provincialism, he saw clearly the "partiality," the lack of universality, in most of our modern literature, and accordingly browsed freely in the delectable fields of the older English poets, of the Classics, and of the Oriental religious books. In the passage from which I have just quoted, Thoreau goes on to deprecate the indifference of Europe to "the poets and philosophers of Persia or of India. . . . Even Goethe wanted that universality of genius which would have appreciated the philosophy of India." If we bear in mind the important distinction that cosmopolitanism has to do with quality perhaps more than with range of interest, there is no reason why we should not pronounce Thoreau's reading cosmopolitan: it was cosmopolitan in range, if not in quality. That is not high praise, but it *is* praise. That Thoreau in all spent only a year of his life outside of the immediate neighborhood of Concord, does not in itself indicate provincialism. Concord, in Thoreau's day, was the center of American culture; in it converged a veritable multitude of influences. If we regard him as provincial, we must, I think, look elsewhere for evidence. At all events in the battle of the books, Thoreau, with something approaching universality (however naive that universality) shunned the moderns and sided with the ancients, even the ancient Hindoos.

To Oriental literature, as has long been recognized, his debt was great. He immersed himself in that literature, especially in the "vast and cosmogonal philosophy of the Bhagvat-Geeta," as in the bracing waters of a newly discovered ocean. In addition to the Bhagvat-Geeta, he read with particular keenness the Vedas, the Vishnu Purana, the Institute of Menu. He liked to speak of the "Scriptures of the nations,"—"the collected Scriptures or Sacred Writings of the several nations, the Chinese, the Hindoos, the Persians, the Hebrews, and others"; these, he believed, ought to be printed together as the true Bible, "which let the missionaries carry to the uttermost parts of the earth." This project bade fair to be approximated by the Transcendental organ, the *Dial,* in which selections from these religious books were published serially, Thoreau himself making the selections. His praise of the Orientals (mainly, always, the Hindoos) may be summed up under two heads: Contemplation and Elevation. The Hindoo philosophers were of course well adapted to our New England period of plain living and high thinking. Impossible to the Calvinist, or to the deist of the eighteenth century, or to the typical Unitarian, they were bread of life to the Transcendentalists, and especially to Thoreau. His introspective and contemplative mind was naturally attracted by the Hindoos: "So many years and ages of the gods those Eastern sages sat contemplating Brahm, uttering in silence the mystic 'Om,' being absorbed into the essence of the Supreme Being, never going out of themselves, but subsiding farther and deeper within"; though they had, certainly, the defect of this virtue: "so infinitely wise, yet infinitely stagnant" (and stagnation is death to a Transcendentalist). Their thought, again, was elevated: nowhere, says Thoreau, is the reader "raised into and sustained in a higher, purer, or *rarer* region of thought than in the Bhagvat-Geeta." In connection with this characteristic elevation might be mentioned their austerity, which has its obvious relation to certain stoical and ascetic instincts in Thoreau: "The very austerity of the Brahmans," he says, "is tempting to the devotional soul, as a more refined pleasure." In 1855, after Thoreau had long been familiar with many of the Eastern books, he received as a gift from his English friend Cholmondeley a collection of these books,—"a royal gift," as he described it, "in the shape of twenty-one distinct works (one in nine volumes,—forty-four volumes in all), almost exclusively relating to ancient Hindoo literature, and scarcely one to be bought in America." This delightful event must have confirmed him in his habit of "recruiting" himself in this literature of Contemplation and Elevation. The next year, on meeting Walt Whitman, who seemed to him "wonderfully like the Orientals," he asked whether he had read them. "No," replied Whitman, "tell me about them"—an incident which illustrates, among other things, the danger one encounters in attributing, not only any of Whitman's but also any of Thoreau's traits to the direct influence of "the Orientals." Rather too much has been made of this influence, as if every hint of a correspondence betokened borrowing. It is near the truth to say that Thoreau went to the religious books of the East because of certain correspondences in him to Eastern modes of thought, than that these Eastern modes of thought produced correspondences in him. As he says himself, "like some other preachers, I have added my texts —derived from the Chinese and Hindoo scriptures—long after my discourse was written."

Far more important than Oriental literature, in the formation of Thoreau's mind and character, is his reading in what might be termed local history, the tradition of the environment in which he lived. Though descended from Puritan ancestors through one parent only, Thoreau was as good a Puritan as any other Transcendentalist, Emerson included; indeed, I believe one would not be wide of the mark in asserting that he was more a Puritan than was Emerson, despite the latter's impressive ancestral relation with the stern, God-fearing men of the early colony. However that may be, his interest in the Puritan tradition is patent. Ardently devoted to the soil on which he was born, Thoreau dwelt on its past almost as eagerly as on its present. Aside from his interest in oral tradition, he read sympathetically in the literature (nearly worthless as literature) that revealed the past of his Concord, his Massachusetts, his New England. The reading that he pursued in this field may be divided into three classes.

The first class is composed of those books, many of them written by the Pilgrim Fathers, that deal with the discovery, settlement, and early annals of Puritan New England. He knew such works as the following: *The History of Plymouth Plantation,* by William Bradford; *The True Travels and Observations of Captain John Smith; Good News from New England,* by Edward Winslow; *History of New England,* by John Winthrop; Mourt's *Relation; New England's Prospect,* by William Wood; *New English Canaan,* by Thomas Morton; *Account of Two Voyages,* by John Josselyn. Most of these mentioned are quoted frequently; some, especially William Wood, discussed at length. He admired the probity of these men of action, their sense of character, their sense of life ("the strong new soil speaks through them"). In *Cape Cod* is an extended account, largely from Mourt, of the landing of the Pilgrims; the *Journal* contains frequent references to the Pilgrims; he apparently relished the description of "a New England November in 1620" as it looked "to Bradford's eyes," for it occurs twice in the *Journal,*—once incorrectly, as if quoted from memory,—and is cited as a true vision of nature (not nature seen from "the gentlemanly windows of the country seat"); everywhere in Thoreau's writings we come face to face with the virile New England of that day, a New England now resurgent in the guise of Transcendentalism—even nature is seen, at times, with a Puritan imagination: "The trees stand with boughs downcast like pilgrims beaten by a storm, and the whole landscape wears a sombre aspect."

The second class of reading in "local history" to some extent overlaps the first,—histories of states and towns: the town history of Concord, of Dunstable, and the like. This kind of reading suggests an even more intense interest in the past of his environment: Thoreau was willing to wade through many a dull chapter, perhaps a whole volume, for the sake of a handful of picturesque or heroic incidents.

Lastly, there is Thoreau's extensive reading in the lore of the North American Indian and other savage peoples. Channing was much impressed with Thoreau's unwonted perseverance in "working up the Indian": "These books," he wrote in his biography, "form a library by themselves. Extracts from reliable authorities from De Bry to poor Schoolcraft, with the early plates and maps accurately copied, and selections from travelers the world over. . . . With the Indian vocabularies he was familiar, and in his Maine excursions tested his knowledge by all the words he could get from the savages *in puris naturalibus.* . . . He read and translated the Jesuit relations of the first Canadian missions, containing 'the commodities and discommodities' of the Indian life, such as the roasting of a fresh parson." In a word, he probably studied the Indian as closely as he ever studied anything. He was familiar with the Indian tradition of New England, as he was with the Puritan. And there was a good deal of the Indian in his constitution, as there was of the Puritan.

Channing thought that Thoreau's taste in English literature was "very exquisite." With some exceptions it assuredly was. While in college he browsed at will in English literature, which to him virtually meant English poetry, singling out as special kindred spirits the writers of Elizabethan England and of the earlier seventeenth century; and in 1843, while living with William Emerson at Staten Island, he utilized the library facilities of New York by extending his readings in this field. In the pre-Elizabethan period he had two boon companions, the Robin Hood ballads and Chaucer, delighting in their health (the morbidly plaintive note in modern literature, rising to a wail in this or that romantic poet, was his aversion). "Chaucer," he writes, "may be regarded as in many respects the English Homer"; he is fresh and young and natural; we admire him, too, for "his sturdy English wit," though that marks his limits, for he "is essentially humorous, as the loftiest genius never is." Ossian might also be mentioned here, since Thoreau placed him in "that misty weather" of a pre-Chaucerian age. The pseudo-grandeur of Ossian quite captured the romanticist in him. In general, however, it is fair to say that

Thoreau came very near restricting himself, in his reading of English literature, to the Elizabethan period and the early seventeenth century. For the literature of the Romantic Movement and of the early Victorian age, as we have noted, he cared little, and even less, perhaps, for the whole stretch from Dryden to Wordsworth, including such writers as Pope and Addison and Burke and Goldsmith, on whom his contemporaries were mainly nourished. But in the lively fancy and healthy imagination of the time of Shakespeare and of Herbert he fairly revelled. Shakespeare himself "I fear he had never finished"—so Channing betrays his friend; possibly Shakespeare had not so palpable a *charm* as some of his lesser coevals. Milton he valued, Channing reports, for his elegance; and adds, "Perhaps 'Lycidas' was his favorite short poem; at least I have heard it most often from his mouth." He had read Daniel attentively, especially his *Musophilus*, and, according to Channing, repeated the following lines perhaps more often than any other (not, I take it, any other of Daniel's, but any other, without restriction):

> Unless above himself he can
> Erect himself, how poor a thing is man.

Quarles he enjoyed with a pure delight. In a letter to Emerson in 1843, he wrote, "Quarles's *Divine Poems* as well as *Emblems* are quite a discovery," and in writing to Mrs. Emerson a month later he expressed his pleasure more fully—indeed, the paragraph on Quarles is half the letter:

> I have been reading lately what of Quarles's poetry I could get. He was a contemporary of Herbert, and a kindred spirit. I think you would like him. It is rare to find one who was so much of a poet and so little of an artist. He wrote long poems, almost epics for length, about Jonah, Esther, Job, Samson, and Solomon, interspersed with meditations after a quite original plan,—Shepherd's Oracles, Comedies, Romances, Fancies, and Meditations,—the quintessence of meditation,—and Enchiridions of Meditation all divine,—and what he calls his Morning Muse; besides prose works as curious as the rest. He was an unwearied Christian, and a reformer of some old school withal. Hopelessly quaint, as if he lived all alone and knew nobody but his wife, who appears to have reverenced him. He never doubts his genius; it is only he and his God in all the world. He used language sometimes as greatly as Shakespeare; and though there is not much straight grain in him, there is plenty of tough, crooked timber. In an age when Herbert is revived, Quarles surely ought not to be forgotten.

The quintessence of meditation with such sincerity and simple faith in following the inner leading, and everywhere a charming antiquarian flavor, formed a combination certain to captivate Thoreau. To tell of other favorites in a field in which all were good friends were needless. The following contrast, however, deserves mention: in the first volume of the *Journal,* whereas he comments on only Gray and Johnson and two or three others in the whole of the eighteenth century, in his chosen period he concerns himself with this portentous list: Thomas Fuller, Bacon, Milton, Shakespeare, Johnson, Aubrey, Raleigh, Herbert, Quarles, Carew, Drummond, Peele, Marlowe, Spenser, Sidney, Drayton, Giles Fletcher, Daniel, Donne, Lovelace. That is certainly not the readings of a mere primitivist, or a misanthrope, or a rebel against tradition. Channing's word, "exquisite," when applied to Thoreau's taste in English literature is perhaps not excessive.

The last, and like the foregoing, one of the most important divisions of Thoreau's reading, is the classics. Despite his insistent comment on Greek and Latin writers, despite his constant reading of Homer in particular, despite his translations from classical authors and his paper on Persius in the *Dial,* little significance has been attached to this aspect of Thoreau's intellectual and spiritual life. Yet it is surely of the highest significance. Thoreau without his classical background would simply not have been Thoreau. Channing's statement is this: "That he was familiar with the classics, and kept up the acquaintance, is shown by his translations of Homer, Aeschylus, Pindar, Anacreon, Aristotle, Pliny, Cato, Columella, and other ancient writers. His *Prometheus Unbound* is said to have been reprinted and used as a 'pony' at Harvard; his version of the *Seven Against Thebes* may have disappeared. Homer and Virgil were his favorites, like the world's." Homer and Virgil, however, he hardly rated equally— Homer was, to Thoreau, by all odds the greatest of poets. He was the literary presiding genius at Walden: "I kept Homer's *Iliad* on my table through the summer." On account of his busy life at the pond (for however much he reflected and mused, he hardly ever wasted an hour), he "looked at his page only now and then," but yet, he says, "I sustained myself by the prospect of such reading in future." The book is, however, full of echoes of the *Iliad,* usually in figurative applications. Homer he found bracing as morning air, and fresh and dewy as the water of Walden Pond. "It is enough," he says, "if Homer but say the sun sets. He is as serene as nature, and we can hardly detect the enthusiasm of the bard. It is as if nature spoke. [What more could a poet of nature say?] He presents to us the simplest pictures of human life, so the child itself can understand them, and the man must not think twice to appreciate his naturalness." "There are few books," he adds, "which are fit to be remembered in our wisest hours, but the Iliad is brightest in the serenest days." Homer and the other poets were his delight, but not Plato and the other

philosophers. Emerson's debt to Plato and the Platonists bulks
ever larger as we study him more carefully: he was a New England
Plato, though that caption will not contain all of him. But his friend,
Thoreau, disliking abstract thought as much as Emerson relished it,
probably had the vaguest conception of the Platonic philosophy (such
as one might gather in talks with Emerson, and from English poets
of the seventeenth century), and scarcely knew Plato at all at first
hand. "His *Dialogues*, which contain what was immortal in him," he
says in *Walden*, "lie on the next shelf, and yet I never read them";
and Channing puts the matter even more sweepingly when he asserts,
"I never knew him to say a good word for Plato." Something of
Plotinus and Jamblichus—"the wise Jamblichus," he calls him—he
knew, and of Cudworth, whom he quotes more than once. But, as
Channing says, "Metaphysics was his adversion"; and more to his
taste than even the poetic Plato and his followers, despite the influence of Emerson, were the ancient poets and dramatists—even the
"farmers," Cato and Varro and Columella. The classical authors of
Thoreau's first book, the *Week*, are Anacreon, Aristotle, Hesiod,
Homer, Jamblichus, Ovid, Persius, Pindar, Plutarch, Pythagoras,
Simonides, Sophocles, Varro, and Virgil. The ancient classics, he insists in *Walden*, must be read in the original. While Emerson gen-
erously advises the use of translations, and declares he would as soon
swim across Charles River when going to Boston as read his books
in the original language when translations exist, Thoreau pronounces
with more Emersonian ocularness, "it is remarkable that no transcript of them has ever been made into any modern tongue, unless
our civilization itself may be regarded as such a transcript." No doubt
both of these assertions suffer from the Transcendental superlative;
but aside from the probability that Thoreau's is nearer the truth than
Emerson's, his is also, more than Emerson's, the utterance of one
who loved dearly and venerated the classics, and who had a fair
understanding of the antique symmetry. The classics went far toward
making Thoreau what he was. In his complex constitution, the humanistic ideal was an important factor. It is true that the Homer
read by a decadent romanticist is a debased Homer, as is the Homer
of the pseudo-classicist. Mere devotion to classical literature is not in
itself a virtue, nor the sign of favorable influence. But Thoreau, owing
mainly to the Puritan strain in him, was well fitted to put to noble
use the humanistic ideal. It affected favorably, not only his literary
art, but also his whole view of life—his attitude toward nature and
toward society.

　Some conception of the relative importance of the various divisions
of Thoreau's reading may be had through an examination of the
poetical quotations in the *Week* (a list of those successfully traced

may be extracted from the appendix). Of classical authors, Homer is quoted six times, Virgil and Pindar each four times, and Ovid twice; of early English, ballads six times, Chaucer four times, and Gower twice; of Elizabethan and seventeenth century, Quarles eight, Daniel six, Spenser five, Marlowe and Donne three each, Charles Cotton, Herbert, Habington, Shakespeare, and Giles Fletcher twice each; of later English and American, Emerson six times, Ellery Channing five, and Tennyson three. Although this list includes only poets, it indicates afresh Thoreau's predilection for the classics and for the English literature of the Elizabethan age and the age immediately following; to complete the record, we should need to add the "local history" reading, especially in New England Puritan writers, the religious books of the Orient, and one or two modern writers such as Wordsworth and Carlyle. Which of these is most important is by no means easy to determine; they are all essential, so much is certain, and perhaps that is enough.

There were serious gaps in Thoreau's reading; his was, as Channing puts it, "a very uncompleted reading." That large and far from negligible department of literary expression which he designated as "fiction," meaning novels, prose tales, and the like, he shunned as steadfastly as any of those benighted Puritans of old whose traits he had absorbed from the air, if not from their blood. "I never read a novel, they have so little real life and thought in them." Again, he made too slight use of that "good knowledge of French" which he had; and his "some acquaintance with Italian, Spanish, and German" was never fostered to anything approaching a state of intimacy but remained little more than a bowing acquaintance. Goethe, for instance, if Thoreau had really assimilated his teachings, would have enlarged his personality, and his outlook on the civilization of modern times, though the gain in centrality might have been in part offset by a loss in eccentricity, in that wild-apple flavor that many readers of Thoreau value above all else in him. Another gap, which has already been noted, is the literature of eighteenth century England, including such names as Burke and Swift and Dr. Johnson, who surely deserved a better hearing than Thoreau gave them. Actually, this gap was still wider; in the entire long procession from Dryden to Matthew Arnold, Thoreau had but a handful of friends.

The gaps are veritable abysses, it is true; but as much may be said of the reading, even of the culture, of most men of genius. On the other hand, the range and thoroughness of Thoreau's acquaintance with literature, all the way from the *Bhagvat-Geeta* to *Sartor Resartus,* are not to be tacitly deprecated, as they have been in the past. He read much and well. "Books," he says, "must be read as deliberately and reservedly as they were written"; and this describes his own habit. What he absorbed unconsciously from his Transcendental environment, he supplemented through the books that chance—and Emerson—brought to him, freely inviting influence. It was one of his first principles that we should act out what we have read—should not let the feeling or thought lie passive and then languish, but rise and act. What he read, Thoreau became.

But no man can be explained in terms of his reading. Perhaps it is less true to say that Thoreau became what he read, than to say that his reading indicated what he was. There was in him, as there is in every man, a personal element that was inborn, that determined largely the direction and degree of growth, that helped him to choose his books and his friends, that, probably more than anything else, made him what he became. An attempt to investigate this personal element would of course bring us, if we pressed on urgently, to biological factors that are shrouded in mystery.

The Organic Structure of *Walden*[1]

by F. O. Matthiessen

Wherever Thoreau turned for fresh confirmation of his belief that true beauty reveals necessity, he saw that 'Nature is a greater and more perfect art,' and that there is a similarity between her operations and man's even in the details and trifles. He held, like Emerson, that 'man's art has wisely imitated those forms into which all matter is most inclined to run, as foliage and fruit.' But Thoreau studied more examples in detail than Emerson did. Any glance from his door could provide him with fresh evidence. The sumach and pine and hickory that surrounded his cabin reminded him of the most graceful sculptural forms. The tracery of frostwork suggested the intricate refinements of design; and when he wanted his basic lesson in Coleridge's distinction between mechanic and organic form, all he had to do was to mould a handful of earth and to note that however separately interesting its particles might be, their relation was one of mere lifeless juxtaposition. In marked contrast was the shape of even 'the simplest and most lumpish fungus,' and the reasons for its fascination crowded upon him: "it is so obviously organic and related to ourselves . . . It is the expression of an idea; growth according to a law; matter not dormant, not raw, but inspired, appropriated by spirit.' With so many principles to be gleaned from the humblest growth, no wonder he held it 'monstrous when one cares but little about trees but much about Corinthian columns.'

When he tried to apply these principles to creation in literature, he sometimes was content with saying that 'true art is but the expression of our love of nature.' But he often pushed to a rigorous extreme not merely the supremacy of nature over art and of content over form, but also that of the artist's life over his work. He developed his own version of Milton's view that the heroic poem could be written only by the man who had lived a heroic life. As Thoreau put it, 'Nothing goes by luck in composition . . . The best you can write will be the

1 Title supplied by the editor.

From American Renaissance: Art and Expression in the Age of Emerson and Whitman *by F. O. Matthiessen. Copyright* © *1941 by Oxford University Press, Inc. Reprinted by permission of the publisher.*

best that you are.' His distrust of 'the *belles lettres* and the *beaux arts* and their professors' sprang from his desire to break down all artificial divisions between art and living. He often confronted the problem that 'it is not easy to write in a journal what interests us at any time, because to write it is not what interests us.' [2] His only solution for this dilemma was, as he said in a letter to one of his followers: 'As for style of writing, if one has anything to say, it drops from him simply and directly, as a stone falls to the ground.' He came to the same point when he praised the style of John Brown: 'The *art* of composition is as simple as the discharge of a bullet from a rifle, and its masterpieces imply an infinitely greater force behind them. This unlettered man's speaking and writing are standard English. Some words and phrases deemed vulgarisms and Americanisms before, he has made standard American.' Again Thoreau was much closer than he knew to Greenough, who had insisted that the style indicated by our mechanics was miscalled economical and cheap. On the contrary, Greenough said, 'It is the dearest of styles . . . Its simplicity is not the simplicity of emptiness or of poverty, its simplicity is that of justness, I had almost said, of justice.'

When Thoreau said, 'Give me simple, cheap, and homely themes,' he had no notion that their execution would prove easy. Even when he declared that the real poem is what the poet himself has become, he added that 'our whole life is taxed for the least thing well done.' In adopting the tenet that poetry consists in knowing the quality of a thing, he had realized by his early thirties that such knowledge could be arrived at only through the slowest unconscious process, for 'at first blush a man is not capable of reporting truth; he must be drenched and saturated with it first. What was *enthusiasm* in the young man must become *temperament* in the mature man.' We might compare this with Lawrence's realization that 'we have to know ourselves pretty thoroughly before we can break through the automatism of ideals and conventions . . . Only through fine delicate knowledge can we recognize and release our impulses.' Only in seasoned maturity, to shift back to Thoreau's imagery, will the poet's truth exhale as naturally from him as 'the odor of the muskrat from the coat of the trapper.'

He often spoke of the organic style in an equally characteristic image—of its being a slow growth, unfolding under the care of the poet's patient hands. The degree to which his own practice lived up to that metaphor is also the degree to which his craftsmanship goes beyond Emerson's. He accepted the older man's view that genius is

---

2 Or as he phrased it in an awkward couplet in the *Week:*
    My life has been the poem I would have writ,
    But I could not both live and utter it.

the abundance of health, but was less intermittent in his demand that talent must go with genius. To be sure, he hardly ever discusses specific forms. He apparently took it for granted that the artist's intuition will shape what is proper for it, and, in the course of objecting to some of Carlyle's extravagances, said little more than that the great writer works not by introducing new forms but by reinvigorating old ones. However, in his perception that this renewal comes through the fresh handling of words, he generally sensed a more integral connection between the words and the thought than Emerson did. That was why he regarded translations as an impossibility, and held that the classics could be read only after a training as rigorous 'as the athletes underwent.' Moreover, he made another discrimination, essentially foreign to Emerson, between the spoken and the written word. He held that 'what is called eloquence in the forum is commonly found to be rhetoric in the study,' that however much we may admire the orator's power, the style that lives beyond the emotion of the moment demands a much more exacting composition. When Thoreau said of the poet, almost in Frost's words, that 'the tone and pitch of his voice is the main thing,' he knew that 'a perfect expression requires a particular rhythm or measure for which no other can be substituted.' Such knowledge—the product, as we have seen, of his own sensitive organization—was his firmest defense against the formlessness that beset his desire to speak in harmony with nature. If it seldom rescued his immature verse—almost the type instance of mechanic form in its imitation of the surface tricks of the metaphysicals—it brought both precision and timbre to the movement of his ripened prose.

Only by the accumulation of such slight threads as those spun out in the last paragraph can we finally distinguish between Thoreau's and Emerson's understanding of the organic style. In Emerson's record of one of the early conversations between them (1838), it was Thoreau who was complaining that 'if the man took too much pains with the expression, he was not any longer the Idea himself.' Emerson agreed, but pointed out 'that this was the tragedy of Art that the artist was at the expense of the man.' However, as the years advanced, it was the younger writer who was to accept this inevitable fact. Observing, two decades later, that farmer Tarbell had at last got his barn built, he knew that the artist could make his structure only through an equally 'steady struggle, with alternate failure and success.' He must learn both endurance and detachment, for his work consists in performing '*post-mortem* examinations of himself before he is dead.' Or, in a different figure, he must have 'the cold skill' to quarry and carve a statue out of his own feelings. This subordination of himself to the work to be done reminds us, even in its phrasing,

of what Eliot has valued in Hawthorne: 'the firmness, the true coldness, the hard coldness of the genuine artist.'

*   *   *

In contrasting Thoreau with Emerson, Alcott felt that the former
revealed secrets of nature 'older than fields and gardens,' that 'he
seems alone, of all the men I have known, to be a native New Eng-
lander.' Yet he could not help regretting at times that Thoreau was
so earthbound, and wished that he might come out of the woods to
the orchards, and so be pastoral instead of wild. It is doubtful whether
most readers now sense in Thoreau more than a whiff of wildness.
He wanted to bring into his writing 'muck from the meadows'; but
what he really managed to bring finds an apter image in the delicate
fragrance of the ferns or perhaps the ranker odor of the pines. His
instinct towards the higher life was so inordinately encouraged by his
contemporaries that it was only by the sturdiest action that he held
fast to the soil. He described his most fertile process while saying why
he went to the woods: 'Let us settle ourselves, and work and wedge our
feet downward through the mud and slush of opinion, and prejudice,
and tradition, and delusion, and appearance, that alluvion which
covers the globe, through Paris and London, through New York and
Boston and Concord, through Church and State, through poetry and
philosophy and religion, till we come to a hard bottom and rocks in
place, which we can call *reality,* and say, This is, and no mistake.'
This positive dredging beat reminds us again of his awareness of
the physical basis of rhythm. It can remind us also of what Lawrence
felt, that 'the promised land, if it be anywhere, lies away beneath
our feet. No more prancing upwards. No more uplift.' Lawrence's discovery was quickened by watching and almost identifying himself
with the downward thrust into the earth of the feet of Indian dancers.
But Thoreau's knowledge was owing less directly to the Indians than
to his re-creation for himself of the conditions of primitive life. He
approximated Lawrence's words when he said that in good writing,
'the poem is drawn out from under the feet of the poet, his whole
weight has rested on this ground.' Emerson, by contrast, wanted to
'walk upon the ground, but not to sink.' What Thoreau's language
gained from his closer contact can be read in his evocation of a river
walk, where every phrase is expressive of acute sensation: "Now your
feet expand on a smooth sandy bottom, now contract timidly on
pebbles, now slump in genial fatty mud, amid the pads."
But as you think again of the prolonged sensuous and rhythmical
experience that Lawrence was able to make out of his response to the
New Mexican corn dance, or of Hemingway's account of fishing on
Big Two-Hearted River, you realize that Thoreau's product was

ordinarily somewhat less full-bodied. When he said, 'Heaven is under our feet as well as over our heads,' he was speaking of the luminous clarity of the pond. A characteristic example to put beside Emerson's 'Snow-Storm' is the poem 'Smoke':

> Light-winged Smoke, Icarian bird,
> Melting thy pinions in thy upward flight,
> Lark without song, and messenger of dawn,
> Circling above the hamlets as thy nest;
> Or else, departing dream, and shadowy form
> Of midnight vision, gathering up thy skirts;
> By night star-veiling, and by day
> Darkening the light and blotting out the sun;
> Go thou my incense upward from this hearth,
> And ask the gods to pardon this clear flame.

The delicacy of the wraith-like movement finds its articulation in the succession of predominantly high-pitched vowels in the opening two lines. The 'Icarian bird,' a neat image for the melting away of the smoke in the bright morning sky, may then lead into too many fanciful conceits, but any tendency to vagueness is checked by the accurate epithet, 'star-veiling.' With that the contrast between the 'shadowy form' and the rays of light, latent from the start, flowers exquisitely and prepares the way for the final statement, which makes the poem no mere descriptive exercise but Thoreau's declaration of his ever fresh renewal of purpose with the kindling of his fire in the morning. The 'clear flame' of his spirit is so distinct and firm that it needs his plea for pardon to keep him from verging on *hubris* as he confidently contrasts his life with a world which is obscure and desperate in its confusion. That full contrast, to be sure, emerges only through the poem's context in *Walden,* but enough of the human situation is implied in the verses themselves to let them serve as a rounded, if minute, instance of Coleridge's distinction between imitation and mere copying. Coleridge held that the artist must not try to make a surface reproduction of nature's details, but 'must imitate that which is within the thing . . . for so only can he hope to produce any work truly natural in the object and truly human in the effect.' That combination has been created in this poem, since the reader's pleasure does not spring from the specific recordings, however accurate, but from the imperceptible interfusion with these of the author's own knowledge and feeling, and of his skill in evolving an appropriate form.

*   *   *

It is apparent, in view of this last distinction of Coleridge's, that the real test of whether Thoreau mastered organic form can hardly be made on the basis of accounting for the differences in body and flavor between his portrayal of the natural world and Emerson's, revelatory as these differences are. Nor can it be made by considering one of the rare occasions when his verse was redeemed by virtue of his discipline in translating from the Greek Anthology. Nor is it enough to reckon with the excellence of individual passages of prose, since the frequent charge is that whereas Emerson was master of the sentence, Thoreau was master of the paragraph, but that he was unable to go farther and attain 'the highest or structural achievements of form in a whole book.' The only adequate way of answering that is by considering the structure of *Walden* as a whole, by asking to what extent it meets Coleridge's demand of shaping, 'as it develops, itself from within.'

On one level *Walden* is the record of a personal experience, yet even in making that remark we are aware that this book does not go rightfully into the category of *Two Years Before the Mast* or *The Oregon Trail.* Why it presents a richer accumulation than either of those vigorous pieces of contemporary history is explained by its process of composition. Although Thoreau said that the bulk of its pages were written during his two years of sojourn by the pond (1845-7), it was not ready for publication until seven years later, and ultimately included a distillation from his journals over the whole period from 1838. A similar process had helped to transform his week's boat trip with his brother from a private to a symbolical event, since the record was bathed in memory for a decade (1839-49) before it found its final shape in words. But the flow of the *Week* is as leisurely and discursive as the bends in the Concord river, and the casual pouring in of miscellaneous poems and essays that Thoreau had previously printed in *The Dial* tends to obscure the cyclical movement. Yet each day advances from dawn to the varied sounds of night, and Thoreau uses an effective device for putting a period to the whole by the shift of the final morning from lazy August to the first sharp forebodings of transforming frost.

The sequence of *Walden* is arranged a good deal more subtly, perhaps because its subject constituted a more central symbol for Thoreau's accruing knowledge of life. He remarked on how the pond itself was one of the earliest scenes in his recollection, dating from the occasion when he had been brought out there one day when he was four, and how thereafter 'that woodland vision for a long time made the drapery of my dreams.' By 1841 he had already announced, 'I want to go soon and live away by the pond,' and when pressed by friends about what he would do when he got there, he had asked in turn if it would not be employment enough 'to watch the progress of the seasons'? In that same year he had said: 'I think I could write a poem to be called "Concord." For argument I should have the River, the Woods, the Ponds, the Hills, the Fields, the Swamps and Meadows, the Streets and Buildings, and the Villagers.' In his completed 'poem' these last elements had receded into the background. What had come squarely to the fore, and made the opening chapter by far the longest of all, was the desire to record an experiment in 'Economy' as an antidote to the 'lives of quiet desperation' that he saw the mass of men leading. This essay on how he solved his basic needs of food and shelter might stand by itself, but also carries naturally forward to the more poignant condensation of the same theme in 'Where I lived, and What I lived for,' which reaches its conclusion in the passage on wedging down to reality.

At this point the skill with which Thoreau evolved his composition begins to come into play. On the one hand, the treatment of his material might simply have followed the chronological outline; on the other, it might have drifted into being loosely topical. At first glance it may appear that the latter is what happened, that there is no real cogency in the order of the chapters. That would have been Lowell's complaint, that Thoreau 'had no artistic power such as controls a great work to the serene balance of completeness.'[3] But so far as the opposite can be proved by the effective arrangement of his entire material, the firmness with which Thoreau binds his successive links is worth examining. The student and observer that he has settled himself to be at the end of his second chapter leads easily into his discussion of 'Reading,' but that in turn gives way to his concern with the more fundamental language, which all things speak, in the chapter on 'Sounds.' Then, after he has passed from the tantivy of wild pigeons to the whistle of the locomotive, he reflects that once the cars have gone by and the restless world with them, he is more alone than ever. That starts the transition to the chapter on 'Solitude,' in which the source of his joy is to live by himself in the midst of

---

[3] The don of Harvard was not entirely blind to the man of Concord. Even in his notorious essay on *Walden* in *My Study Windows* he perceived that Thoreau 'had caught his English at its living source, among the poets and prose-writers of its best days,' and compared him with Donne and Browne. When Lowell tried to dismiss Thoreau as a crank, he was really bothered, as Henry Canby has pointed out, by Thoreau's attack upon his own ideals of genteel living. How different from Emerson's is Lowell's tone when he says that while Thoreau 'studied with respectful attention the minks and woodchucks, his neighbors, he looked with utter contempt on the august drama of destiny of which his country was the scene, and on which the curtain had already risen.' As Mr. Canby has added: 'By destiny, Lowell clearly means the "manifest destiny" of the exploitation of the West, whose more sordid and unfortunate aspects Thoreau had prophesied two generations before their time of realization.'

nature with his senses unimpaired. The natural contrast is made in the next chapter on 'Visitors,' which he opens by saying how he believes he loves society as much as most, and is ready enough to fasten himself 'like a bloodsucker for the time to any full-blooded man' who comes his way. But after he has talked enthusiastically about the French woodchopper, and other welcome friends from the village, he remembers 'restless committed men,' the self-styled reformers who felt it their duty to give him advice. At that he breaks away with 'Meanwhile my beans . . . were impatient to be hoed'; and that opening carries him back to the earlier transition to the chapter on 'Sounds': 'I did not read books the first summer; I hoed beans.'

The effect of that repetition is to remind the reader of the time sequence that is knitting together all these chapters after the building of the cabin in the spring. From 'The Bean Field' as the sphere of his main occupation, he moves on, in 'The Village,' to his strolls for gossip, which, 'taken in homeopathic doses, was really as refreshing in its way as the rustle of leaves and the peeping of frogs.' Whether designedly or not, this chapter is the shortest in the book, and yields to rambles even farther away from the community than Walden, to 'The Ponds' and to fishing beyond 'Baker Farm.' As he was returning through the woods with his catch, and glimpsed in the near dark a woodchuck stealing across his path, then came the moment when he 'felt a strange thrill of savage delight, and was strongly tempted to seize and devour him raw.' And in the flash of his realization of his double instinct towards the spiritual and the wild, he has the starting point for the next two contrasting chapters, 'Higher Laws' and 'Brute Neighbors,' in considering both of which he follows his rule of going far enough to please his imagination.

From here on the structure becomes cyclical, his poem of the seasons or myth of the year. The accounts of his varied excursions have brought him to the day when he felt that he could no longer warm himself by the embers of the sun, which 'summer, like a departed hunter, had left.' Consequently he set about finishing his cabin by building a chimney, and called that act 'House-Warming.' There follows a solid block of winter in the three chapters, 'Winter Visitors,' 'Winter Animals,' and 'The Pond in Winter,' that order suggesting the way in which the radius of his experience contracted then more and more to his immediate surroundings. However, the last pages on the pond deal with the cutting of the ice, and end with that sudden extraordinary expansion of his thought which annihilates space and time.

The last movement is the advance to 'Spring.' The activity of the ice company in opening its large tracts has hastened the break-up of the rest of the pond; and, listening to its booming, he recalls that one attraction that brought him to the woods was the opportunity and leisure to watch this renewal of the world. He has long felt in his observations that a day is an epitome of a year, and now he knows that a year is likewise symbolical of a life; and so, in presenting his experience by the pond, he foreshortens and condenses the twenty-six months to the interval from the beginning of one summer to the next. In the melting season he feels more than ever the mood of expanding promise, and he catches the reader up into this rich forward course by one of his most successful kinesthetic images, which serves to round out his cycle: 'And so the seasons went rolling on into summer, as one rambles into higher and higher grass.' To that he adds only the bare statement of when he left the woods, and a 'Conclusion,' which explains that he did so for as good a reason as he had gone there. He had other lives to live, and he knew now that he could find for himself 'a solid bottom everywhere.' That discovery gave him his final serene assurance that 'There is more day to dawn,' and consequently he was not to be disturbed by the 'confused *tintinnabulum*' that sometimes reached his midday repose. He recognized it for the noise of his contemporaries.

The construction of the book involved deliberate rearrangement of material. For instance, a single afternoon's return to the pond in the fall of 1852 was capable of furnishing details that were woven into half a dozen pages of the finished work, two of them separated by seventy pages. Nevertheless, since no invention was demanded, since all the material was a *donnée* of Thoreau's memory, my assertion that *Walden* does not belong with the simple records of experience may require more establishing. The chief clue to how it was transformed into something else lies in Thoreau's extension of his remark that he did not believe himself to be 'wholly involved in Nature.' He went on to say that in being aware of himself as a human entity, he was 'sensible of a certain doubleness' that made him both participant and spectator in any event. This ability to stand 'as remote from myself as from another' is the indispensable attribute of the dramatist. Thoreau makes you share in the excitement of his private scenes, for example, by the kind of generalized significance he can give to his purchase and demolishment of an old shanty for its boards:

I was informed treacherously by a young Patrick that neighbor Seeley, an Irishman, in the intervals of the carting, transferred the still tolerable, straight, and drivable nails, staples, and spikes to his pocket, and then stood when I came back to pass the time of day, and look freshly up, unconcerned, with spring thoughts, at the devastation; there being a dearth of work, as he said. He was there to represent spectatordom, and help make this seemingly insignificant event one with the removal of the gods of Troy.

The demands he made of great books are significant of his own intentions: 'They have no cause of their own to plead, but while they enlighten and sustain the reader his common sense will not refuse them.' Propaganda is not the source of the inner freedom they offer to the reader, for their relation to life is more inclusive than argument; or, as Thoreau described it, they are at once 'intimate' and 'universal.' He aimed unerringly to reconcile these two extremes in his own writing. His experience had been fundamental in that it had sprung from his determination to start from obedience to the rudimentary needs of a man who wanted to be free. Greenough had seen how, in that sense, 'Obedience is worship,' for by discerning and following the functional patterns of daily behavior, you could discover the proportions of beauty that would express and complete them. It was Thoreau's conviction that by reducing life to its primitive conditions, he had come to the roots from which healthy art must flower, whether in Thessaly or Concord. It was not just a figure of speech when he said that 'Olympus is but the outside of the earth everywhere.' The light touch of his detachment allows the comparison of his small things with great, and throughout the book enables him to possess the universe at home.

As a result *Walden* has spoken to men of widely differing convictions, who have in common only the intensity of their devotion to life. It became a bible for many of the leaders of the British labor movement after Morris. When the sound of a little fountain in a shop window in Fleet Street made him think suddenly of lake water, Yeats remembered also his boyhood enthusiasm for Thoreau. He did not leave London then and go and live on Innisfree. But out of his loneliness in the foreign city he did write the first of his poems that met with a wide response, and 'The Lake Isle'—despite its Pre-Raphaelite flavor—was reminiscent of *Walden* even to 'the small cabin' Yeats built and the 'bean rows' he planted in his imagination. *Walden* was also one of our books that bulked largest for Tolstoy when he addressed his brief message to America (1901) and urged us to rediscover the greatness of our writers of the fifties: 'And I should like to ask the American people why they do not pay more attention to these voices (hardly to be replaced by those of financial and industrial millionaires, or successful generals and admirals), and continue the good work in which they made such hopeful progress.' In 1904 Proust wrote to the Comtesse de Noailles: 'Lisez . . . les pages admirables de *Walden*. Il me semble qu'on les lise en soi-même tant elles sortent du fond de notre expérience intime.' 4

In his full utilization of his immediate resources Thoreau was the kind of native craftsman whom Greenough recognized as the har-

4 ["Read . . . the admirable pages of *Walden*. It seems to me that one reads them in oneself because they come from the depths of our intimate experience."]

binger of power for our arts. Craftsmanship in this sense involves the mastery of traditional modes and skills; it has been thought of more often in connection with Indian baskets or Yankee tankards and hearth-tools than with the so-called fine arts. In fact, until fairly lately, despite Greenough's pioneering, it has hardly been consistently thought of in relation to American products of any kind. The march of our experience has been so dominantly expansive, from one rapid disequilibrium to the next, that we have neglected to see what Constance Rourke, among others, has now pointed out so effectively: that notwithstanding the inevitable restlessness of our long era of pioneering, at many stages within that process the strong counter-effort of the settlers was for communal security and permanence. From such islands of realization and fulfilment within the onrushing torrent have come the objects, the order and balance of which now, when we most need them, we can recognize as among the most valuable possessions of our continent. The conspicuous manifestation of these qualities, as Greenough already knew, has been in architecture as the most social of forms, whether in the clipper, or on the New England green, or in the Shaker communities. But the artifacts of the cabinet maker, the potter and the founder, or whatever other utensils have been shaped patiently and devotedly for common service, are likewise a testimony of what Miss Rourke has called our classic art, recognizing that this term 'has nothing to do with grandeur, that it cannot be copied or imported, but is the outgrowth of a special mode of life and feeling.'

Thoreau's deep obligation to such traditional ways has been obscured by our thinking of him only as the extreme protestant. It is now clear that his revolt was bound up with a determination to do all he could to prevent the dignity of common labor from being degraded by the idle tastes of the rich. When he objected that 'the mason who finishes the cornice of the palace returns at night perchance to a hut not so good as a wigwam,' he showed the identity of his social and aesthetic foundations. Although he did not use Greenough's terms, he was always requiring a functional relationship. What he responded to as beauty was the application of trained skill to the exigencies of existence. He made no arbitrary separation between arts, and admired the Indian's woodcraft or the farmer's thorough care in building a barn on the same grounds that he admired the workmanship of Homer.[5] The depth to which his ideals for fitness

[5] Emerson also said, 'I like a man who likes to see a fine barn as well as a good tragedy.' And Whitman added, as his reaction to the union of work and culture, 'I know that pleasure filters in and oozes out of me at the opera, but I know too that subtly and unaccountably my mind is sweet and odorous within while I clean up my boots and grease the pair that I reserve for stormy weather.'

and beauty in writing were shaped, half unconsciously, by the modes of productive labor with which he was surrounded, or, in fact, by the work of his own hands in carpentry or pencil-making or gardening, can be read in his instinctive analogies. He knew that the only discipline for Canning's 'sublimo-slipshod style' would be to try to carve some truths as roundly and solidly as a stonecutter. He knew it was no good to write, 'unless you feel strong in the knees.' Or—a more unexpected example to find in him—he believed he had learned an important lesson in design from the fidelity with which the operative in the textile-factory had woven his piece of cloth.

The structural wholeness of *Walden* makes it stand as the firmest product in our literature of such life-giving analogies between the processes of art and daily work. Moreover, Thoreau's very lack of invention brings him closer to the essential attributes of craftsmanship, if by that term we mean the strict, even spare, almost impersonal 'revelation of the object,' in contrast to the 'elaborated skill,' the combinations of more variegated resources that we describe as technique. This contrast of terms is still Miss Rourke's, in distinguishing between kinds of painting, but it can serve equally to demonstrate why Thoreau's book possesses such solidity in contrast, say, with *Hiawatha* or *Evangeline*. Longfellow was much the more obviously gifted in his available range of forms and subject matters. But his graceful derivations from his models—the versification and gentle tone of Goethe's *Hermann and Dorothea* for *Evangeline*, or the metre of the *Kalevala* for *Hiawatha*—were not brought into fusion with his native themes.[6] Any indigenous strength was lessened by the reader's always being conscious of the metrical dexterity as an ornamental exercise. It is certainly not to be argued that technical proficiency must result in such dilutions, but merely that, as Greenough saw, it was very hard for American artists of that day, who had no developed tradition of their own, not to be thus swamped by their contact with European influences. Their very aspiration for higher standards of art than those with which they were surrounded tended to make them think of form as a decorative refinement which could be imported.

The particular value of the organic principle for a provincial society thus comes into full relief. Thoreau's literal acceptance of Emerson's proposition that vital form 'is only discovered and executed by the artist, not arbitrarily composed by him,' impelled him to minute inspection of his own existence and of the intuitions that rose from it. Although this involved the restriction of his art to parochial limits,

6 And as F. L. Pattee has said of *Hiawatha*, in *The Feminine Fifties* (1940): 'The only really Indian thing about the poem is the Indian summer haze that softens all its outlines, but even this atmosphere is Indian only in name: it was borrowed from German romantic poets.'

to the portrayal of man in terms only of the immediate nature that drew him out, his study of this interaction also brought him to fundamental human patterns unsuspected by Longfellow. Thoreau demonstrated what Emerson had merely observed, that the function of the artist in society is always to renew the primitive experience of the race, that he 'still goes back for materials and begins again on the most advanced stage.' Thoreau's scent for wildness ferreted beneath the merely conscious levels of cultivated man. It served him, in several pages of notes about a debauched muskrat hunter (1859), to uncover and unite once more the chief sources for his own art. He had found himself heartened by the seemingly inexhaustible vitality of this battered character, 'not despairing of life, but keeping the same rank and savage hold on it that his predecessors have for so many generations, while so many are sick and despairing.' Thoreau went on, therefore, half-playfully to speculate what it was that made this man become excited, indeed inspired by the January freshet in the meadows:

> There are poets of all kinds and degrees, little known to each other. The Lake School is not the only or the principal one. They love various things. Some love beauty, and some love rum. Some go to Rome, and some go a-fishing, and are sent to the house of correction once a month . . . I meet these gods of the river and woods with sparkling faces (like Apollo's) late from the house of correction, it may be carrying whatever mystic and forbidden bottles or other vessels concealed, while the dull regular priests are steering their parish rafts in a prose mood. What care I to see galleries full of representatives of heathen gods, when I can see natural living ones by an infinitely superior artist, without perspective tube? If you read the Rig Veda, oldest of books, as it were, describing a very primitive people and condition of things, you hear in their prayers of a still older, more primitive and aboriginal race in their midst and round about, warring on them and seizing their flocks and herds, infesting their pastures. Thus is it in another sense in all communities, and hence the prisons and police.

The meandering course of Thoreau's reflections here should not obscure his full discovery that the uneradicated wildness of man is the anarchical basis both of all that is most dangerous and most valuable in him. That he could dig down to the roots of primitive poetry without going a mile from Concord accounts for his ability to create 'a true Homeric or Paphlagonian man' in the likeness of the French woodchopper. It also helps account for the fact that by following to its uncompromising conclusion his belief that great art can grow from the center of the simplest life, he was able to be universal. He had understood that in the act of expression a man's whole being, and his natural and social background as well, function organically together. He had mastered a definition of art akin to what Maritain has extracted from scholasticism: *Recta ratio factibilium,* the right ordering of the thing to be made, the right revelation of the material.

The Movement of Thoreau's Prose

by John C. Broderick

> Our voyaging is only great-circle sailing.
> *Walden*
>
> Our expeditions are but tours, and come round
> again at evening to the old hearth-side from which
> we set out. Half the walk is but retracing our steps.
> "Walking"

Although Henry David Thoreau clearly aimed such barbs as these at the unadventurous sojourner in life, the quotations fairly describe the pattern of his own walks, the history of his life, and even—I venture to suggest—the pattern of his most characteristic prose and the structure of some of his controlling ideas.

I

A geometric design of the life of Thoreau would run to loops and curlicues. Concord was home base for a series of forays into the larger, more or less alien world. These began as practical *ad hoc* ventures: a pencil-selling trip to New York, interim teaching in Canton, Massachusetts, the four-year Harvard enterprise itself, designed to fit him for the great world and thus perhaps to disqualify him for Concord. That Henry—and not his brother John—should have been the beneficiary of family sacrifices is curious, and Thoreau himself is reported to have said that his education was not worth its cost. Whatever the family hopes and whatever his own evaluation, Harvard did not entirely "take" with Thoreau. During his freshman year, he walked home from Cambridge, the last two miles in his stocking feet. And when at the end of four years he returned to Concord, better shod and clutching the diploma a misinformed posterity has sought to deny him, he was—though he may not have realized it then—home to stay.

He may not have realized it, for the young graduate busily set out

"The Movement of Thoreau's Prose," by John C. Broderick. *From* American Literature, *XXXIII (May, 1961), 133-42. Copyright* © *1961 by Duke University Press. Reprinted by permission of the publisher.*

his trotlines for employment, and one who knew him well said that he would have gone to Alexandria, Virginia, to teach "if accepted." Nevertheless, there soon appeared a nagging, if only partly conscious, reluctance to leave his native town for more than a short excursion. Shortly before he left college Mrs. Thoreau had advised her son to "roam abroad to seek your fortune." His eyes filled with tears, but his sister Helen kissed him and spoke comfortingly, "No, Henry. You shall not go. You shall stay at home and live with us."[1] And so he did. His longest subsequent absence from Concord occurred in 1843 during his perfunctory and unhappy assault on the literary capital of New York at the urging of his patron, Emerson. It was conspicuously unsuccessful, and perhaps made Thoreau the readier the next year to decline a friend's invitation to visit Europe.

The outings made memorable for literature had begun in 1839 when Henry and John Thoreau spent a week on the Concord and Merrimac rivers. Others followed: to Wachusett, to Cape Cod, to Maine, to Canada, most memorably to Walden Pond. The river voyage initiated the pulsations of departure and return prominent especially in the years after Walden. Thoreau made the excursions of the 1850's with his eye on the periodical market, no doubt, but an excursion to Maine was an excursion merely, defined by return to Concord, whereas the ambitious venture to Staten Island had threatened to become linear, not circular. Concord, "the most estimable place in all the world," was his locus of value, periodic departures from which were followed by symmetrical returns.

The Concord he loved was, of course, not the tiny village but the spacious "town." When the restless 1840's ended with the failure of his first book, Thoreau settled into a routine of daily existence, the high moment of which was the afternoon walk to Conantum, to White Pond, to Walden. "Set out at 3 P.M. for Nine-Acre Corner Bridge *via* Hubbard's Bridge and Conantum, returning *via* Dashing Brook, rear of Baker's, and railroad at 6:30 P.M."[2] So goes a representative passage in Thoreau's *Journal*, the literary monument of the normal life of the 1850's. Excursions outside the township supplied the travel books; daily excursions within it supplied the *Journal*. It is said that the amount of his daily writing in his *Journal* was equivalent to the length of his daily walk.

As for the longer excursions, only at Walden and on the rivers did Thoreau achieve ideal rapport between physical and spiritual. The river voyage was mental as well as literal, but, as study of Thoreau's

---

[1] The anecdote is told by William Ellery Channing in *Thoreau the Poet-Naturalist* (Boston, 1902), p. 18.

[2] Henry David Thoreau, *Writings*, Walden Ed. (Boston and New York, 1906), VIII, 307.

revisions has shown, speculation was rooted in the sheer hard facts of the 1839 voyage. At Walden Thoreau soared because he first came "to know beans." The walk or the successful excursion was thus the factual grounding, the means of spiritual release, and often the literary symbol for their fusion.

II

Thoreau's writings, like *Leaves of Grass,* are full of movement, are on the go. The "walk" supplies structural thread for "Walking," "A Walk to Wachusett," "A Winter Walk," and *Cape Cod.* The extended walk or "journey" serves for *The Maine Woods, A Week on the Concord and Merrimack Rivers,* a "water walk" with occasional scrambling along the bank. Even "Civil Disobedience" records what its author calls "a long journey," the result of "traveling into a far country," and the dislocations of life arraigned in "Slavery in Massachusetts" symbolically culminate in this: "The remembrance of my country spoils my walk." (The surprisingly optimistic conclusion of the latter essay is occasioned by a white water-lily, "the emblem of purity," discovered on a walk.) *Walden* itself might be regarded as a year-long walk, for as in his daily walk Thoreau moved away from the mundane world of the village toward one of heightened awareness and potentiality, only to return spiritually reinvigorated, so *Walden* records an adventuring on life which structurally starts from and returns to the world of quiet desperation.

Thoreau has rarely received credit for such compositional excellence in large matters. James Russell Lowell spoke of his inability to sustain a work "to the serene balance of completeness" while praising his "exquisite mechanical skill" in the sentence or the paragraph.[3] The distinction has remained viable, despite considerable recent interest in Thoreau's structures. His writing is still likely to be described by friendly critics as a "mosaic" or "montage." One of the best, while comparing the writing to "an Indian's quiet tread, covering ground, making distance," nonetheless considers Thoreau "essentially an aphorist whose unit of writing was the epigrammatic sentence."[4] Thoreau's best paragraphs, however, do not depend entirely on "the personality of the writer" for their unity. Instead, they move as Thoreau did and as his books do—from the mundane known to the transcendent knowable and back again. By various stylistic means he involves the reader in an intense spiritual experience, only to set him down again in the world from which he has been removed, presumably with more abundant resources for living.

[3] James Russell Lowell, *Writings,* Riverside Ed. (Boston and New York, 1892), I, 370.
[4] Reginald L. Cook, *Passage to Walden* (Boston, 1949), pp. 220-225.

A fairly simple example of such writing is the first paragraph of *Walden:*

> When I wrote the following pages, or rather the bulk of them, I lived alone, in the woods, a mile from any neighbor, in a house which I had built myself, on the shore of Walden Pond, in Concord, Massachusetts, and earned my living by the labor of my hands only. I lived there two years and two months. At present I am a sojourner in civilized life again.[5]

The paragraph begins deceptively, especially since the disarming qualification, "or rather the bulk of them," suggests a characteristic fastidiousness about fact which authenticates *Walden* as a whole. But the remainder of the first sentence comprises a series of short phrasal units, all but one of which ("in Concord, Massachusetts") puts the "I" at greater and greater remoteness from the world of the ordinary reader, removed by solitude, by locality, by personal construction of his dwelling, and by activity—manual labor. The last two sentences of the paragraph mark the return. The second sentence suggests that the distancing experience had temporal limits (a suggestion implicit in the first three words of the paragraph; we have also been reassured by "Concord, Massachusetts"). The last sentence "places" the "I," but there is ambiguity in the word "sojourner," suggesting that his return may be only temporary, that like Melville's Bulkington he may soon ship on another voyage, that he has not passively renewed ordinary obligations. The paragraph, in short, is a miniature of *Walden* as a whole.

In its "out-and back" movement the paragraph is typical, but in its simplicity of means it is less so. Many of Thoreau's paragraphs have the same movement but employ more complicated devices. Such paragraphs often begin with deceptively simple, largely monosyllabic utterances which are succeeded by poetic, allusive, metaphorical enrichment before the return. But the closing sentence—often humorous—serves two functions: it completes the release, but it also recalls the journey just completed. Meanwhile, during the journey Thoreau has kept his reader aware of starting point and destination. Puns, irony, quirky quotations and allusions, careful etymologies—these are a few of his devices to relieve some of the tension of the journey and forecast release from its spiritual intensity.

The most concentrated example of such writing may be an amusing, rather trivial paragraph near the end of "Economy" in *Walden:*

> Not long since I was present at the auction of a deacon's effects, for his life had not been ineffectual:—
> "The evil that men do lives after them."

[5] *Writings,* II, 3.

As usual, a great proportion was trumpery which had begun to accumulate in his father's day. Among the rest was a dried tapeworm. And now, after lying half a century in his garret and other dust holes, these things were not burned; instead of a *bonfire,* or purifying destruction of them, there was an *auction,* or increasing of them. The neighbors eagerly collected to view them, bought them all, and carefully transported them to their garrets and dust holes, to lie there till their estates are settled, when they will start again. When a man dies he kicks the dust.[6]

The spiritual exhortation of the paragraph is slight, emerging chiefly from the negative examples of "desperation" concerning furnishings. But almost all the devices are here: the pun ("ineffectual"), the familiar quotation eccentrically used, the etymologically exact play on *auction* and *bonfire.* The sheer ingenuity of these words and phrases prompts a double response, in which amusement softens the ardors of the better life and actually secures these ardors a hearing. But the most effective sentence is the last, in which the familiar folk remark cuts two ways. Its familiarity is reassuring (even the low-keyed demands of this paragraph are ultimately impracticable). But its metaphoric aptness ("dust" is a favorite term of Thoreau's for what is wrong with life) sets up reverberations which echo the demands for a life of sanity and principle, even at the moment of release from absolute insistence upon it.

One of the most justly famous passages in *Walden* is that sublime apologia for life in the woods.

I went to the woods because I wished to live deliberately, to front only the essential facts of life, and see if I could not learn what it had to teach, and not, when I came to die, discover that I had not lived. I did not wish to live what was not my life, living is so dear; nor did I wish to practise resignation, unless it was quite necessary. I wanted to live deep and suck out all the marrow of life, to live so sturdily and Spartanlike as to put to rout all that was not life, to cut a broad swath and shave close, to drive life into a corner, and reduce it to its lowest terms, and, if it proved to be mean, why then to get the whole and genuine meanness of it, and publish its meanness to the world; or if it were sublime, to know it by experience, and be able to give a true account of it in my next excursion. For most men, it appears to me, are in a strange uncertainty about it, whether it is of the devil or of God, and have *somewhat hastily* concluded that it is the chief end of man here to "glorify God and enjoy him forever." [7]

An intense paragraph like this provides little comfort for the man

6 *Writings,* II, 75.
7 *Writings,* II, 100-101.

unwilling to accept the most strenuous demands of the moral life; but there is some. The first sentence, like its author, begins deliberately, then mounts and mounts—to an ironic climax. The ultimate distinction of the idealist between "life" and "not life" is nonetheless presented in a verbally playful way. The slightly humorous qualifications of the next sentence ("living is so dear" and "unless it was quite necessary") provide additional momentary relief before we are confronted with that remarkable series of metaphors for life at its best. We have passed Conantum and Nine-Acre Corner now; we are at Walden itself. The language which records the author's fronting of life at "its lowest terms" (really the highest) has forced the reader to a similar fronting. The excitement, the challenge, the appeal are almost unbearable. But we cannot live at Walden forever. To perpetuate such godlike moments would require transfiguration of the human condition. Mercifully, the author initiates a return by the parallel qualifications, "if it proved to be . . . or if it were. . . ." The jocularity of "my next excursion" distances both author and reader from the epiphany only recently shared. The joke continues with the powerful extravagance of the next sentence (ironically balanced by the modest "it appears to me"), but the last words of the paragraph are "glorify God and enjoy him forever," words almost meaningless in their reassuring familiarity. The sojourner through this paragraph, however, has had a glimpse of the glory itself, and for him life (and the stale quotation) can never be exactly the same as before he entered the woods.

The long paragraph following this one in *Walden* reveals other stylistic means of departure and safe return: playful allusions to classical myth and fable (ants and men, pygmies and cranes) and the straight-faced drollery connected with the extended pun on "sleepers." Between these is the almost strident recommendation of "simplicity." In such a passage as that on simplicity, Thoreau loses some of the aesthetic detachment which he elsewhere maintains, but his functional stylistic devices enable the reader, at least, to enter and leave the paragraph with profit and without embarrassment. The companion passage in "Conclusion" in *Walden* ("I left the woods . . ." and the paragraph following) has roughly the same movement, out and back, culminating: "If you have built castles in the air, your work need not be lost; that is where they should be. Now put the foundations under them." Here we emerge almost with a blueprint for approximating in ordinary life the glimpsed reality in art of Romantic idealism.

And there are similar passages: such familiar paragraphs in *Walden* as those beginning "The mass of men lead lives of quiet desperation" ("Economy") and "With thinking we may be beside ourselves in a sane sense" ("Solitude"); that in *A Week* beginning "The New Testament is an invaluable book" ("Sunday"); the paragraph in "Walking" from which the epigraph is taken; and others. Thoreau's highly charged polemical writing ("Civil Disobedience," "Slavery in Massachusetts," and "A Plea for Captain John Brown"), on the other hand, has many paragraphs in which the author provides a journey without a return, working instead toward a more conventional climax. And, needless to say, a great many paragraphs do not reveal this kind of movement at all. But a surprising amount of Thoreau's best remembered and most effective writing through analysis displays its stylistic kinship to the well-loved walk.

Walden as a whole has recently surrendered its dynamic structural secret, in which the movement of the book is associated with the rhythm of the seasons. Still obscure, however, is the nature of some subordinate "movements," embracing several chapters. For example, after explaining where "I" lived and what "I" lived for, Thoreau treats first "Reading," an activity closely associated with civilized life, moves next to "Sounds," many of which still remind him of the village but which progressively and inexorably lead him (and us) further and further into the intense, distancing experience available in "Solitude," which culminates in the account of mystical visits from "the old settler and original proprietor," God himself. An almost too startling return from this high moment begins in the next chapter, "Visitors," the first paragraph of which incongruously, we almost feel *irreverently*, associates the saintly hero of *Walden* with a "bar-room." And the return is completed two chapters later in "The Village," a momentary return (the shortest chapter in *Walden*) before renewing the memorable journey.

At the very center of *Walden* is a troublesome but important chapter called "Higher Laws," which re-echoes some of the objectionable stridency of earlier passages. It nevertheless clearly contains a very intense spiritual exhortation in which fishing is associated with the primitive or wild and the renunciation of animal food with the spiritual or higher nature. The next chapter, "Brute Neighbors," commences with a comic, ironic dialogue between Poet and Hermit, in which the hermit must choose between going "to heaven or a-fishing." He eventually casts for the latter, sure that there "never is but one opportunity of a kind." Astute readers have recognized here some kind of descent, but this particular descent is merely one more example of the Thoreauvian "return" since the ironic dialogue is a comic version of the dualism so stridently insisted on in "Higher Laws." The function of the irony of self-disparagement here and elsewhere is to relax the tensions of the earlier chapter and enable the reader to return, chastened and invigorated but not left in the air of the inhuman abstraction of an impossible dualism.

It is of some interest that these two patterned side trips off the main itinerary of *Walden* cannot be discovered in the first prospectus, the earliest version of the book as reconstructed by J. Lyndon Shanley.[8] That first version lacks also "Conclusion" and thus lacks the ultimate return from Walden with its poignant admission: "I do not say that John or Jonathan will realize all this." In fact, almost none of the specimen passages cited above appear in the "first" *Walden*. Their absence suggests that whatever else Thoreau did with his masterpiece between 1847 and 1854, he discovered the possibilities of a pulsating, dynamic style which would engage the reader, secure his willing suspension of inertia, and involve him in a series of literary journeys seemingly of the greatest import, but not journeys without end.

In style as well as structure, in language as well as idea, then, Thoreau recapitulates the archetypal Romantic theme of rebirth. His significant contribution to the theme is his recognition that the moment of spiritual rebirth is not infinite, that the walk cannot be prolonged indefinitely, that return is inevitable. To death and rebirth, he adds re-entry. In a way, readers of Thoreau have always sensed this characteristic, seeking, however, to define it in philosophical or ethical terms, "the poet-naturalist," for example. But Thoreau, we must remember, is a literary artist, whose service to philosophy and ethics is to provide a fresh literary experience of perhaps old ideas and values. At its best his writing renews the vitality of a life of principle by providing the reader vicarious participation in a compelling version. His rhetorically extreme and seemingly intransigent claims for such a life, however, carry their own ironic qualification and thus make it available as ideal reality, if not as normal actuality.

Thoreau the man had his forbidding rigidities and intransigencies, of course, and Thoreau the almost priggish letter-writer even more. Such static intransigency does pop up now and then in the writing on "simplicity" or "Higher Laws" and occasionally threatens to dominate an entire work, "Life Without Principle," but only rarely. More often the wit, the humor, the irony render Romantic idealism accessible as a guide to life at its best rather than a monstrous abstraction existentially, perhaps, worthless.

The companions of Henry Thoreau's literary walks achieve a concrete experience of Romantic idealism, perhaps ultimately inaccessible in any other way. The dynamism of Thoreau's best writing takes us momentarily out of ourselves to that heaven-approaching plane from

---

[8] *The Making of Walden* (Chicago, 1957).

which the world of normality is seen and judged. We are reluctant to depart and, once there, perhaps more reluctant to return. The movement of Thoreau's probe enables us to do both and thus extract the maximum benefit from both the going and the coming back.

Paradox in *Walden*

by *Joseph J. Moldenhauer*

I fear chiefly lest my expression may not be extra-vagant *enough, may not wander far enough beyond the narrow limits of my daily experience, so as to be adequate to the truth of which I have been convinced. Extravagance! it depends on how you are yarded. . . . I desire to speak somewhere without bounds; like a man in a waking moment, to men in their waking moments; for I am convinced that I cannot exaggerate enough even to lay the foundation of a true expression.*[1]

I

The idiosyncrasies of Thoreau's personality and opinions are so absorbing that "paradox" has always been a key term in Thoreau scholarship. Critic of government and relentless reporter of tortoises, Platonic dreamer and statistician of tree rings, Transcendental friend who calls for "pure hate" to underprop his love,[2] Thoreau invites description as paradoxical, enigmatic, or even perverse. But as Joseph Wood Krutch maintains, "to unite without incongruity things ordinarily thought of as incongruous *is* the phenomenon called Thoreau."[3] In *Walden* this propensity toward the resolved contradiction may be observed in full flower. Here Thoreau talks only of himself, yet "brag[s] for humanity." Self-isolated in a spot as remote, he says, as Cassiopeia's Chair, he strolls to the village "every day or two." Renouncing materialism for a poetic and mystic life, he proudly reports his own prudential efficiency, and documents his "economic" success with balance sheets. Bewailing the limitations of science, he

"Paradox in Walden." Reprinted, with the author's revisions, from "The Extravagant *Maneuver: Paradox in* Walden*," The Graduate Journal, VI (Winter, 1964), 132-46. Copyright © 1964 by The Graduate Journal. Reprinted by permission of the author and publisher.*

[1] *The Writings of Henry David Thoreau*, Walden Edition, 20 vols. (Boston, 1906), II *(Walden)*, 357.

[2] *Ibid.*, I, 305. See Perry Miller, *Consciousness in Concord* (Boston, 1958), pp. 80-103, for a full examination of the paradoxes in Transcendental friendship.

[3] Joseph Wood Krutch, *Henry David Thoreau* (New York, 1948), p. 286.

74   *Joseph J. Moldenhauer*

painstakingly measures the depth of the pond and counts the bubbles
in its ice.

The dominant stylistic feature of *Walden* is paradox—paradox in
such quantity and of such significance that we are reminded of the
works of Donne, Sir Thomas Browne, and other English metaphysical
writers. Thoreau's paradoxical assertion—for instance, "Much is published, but little printed"—seems self-contradictory and opposed to
reason. As a poetic device it has intimate connections with metaphor,
because it remains an absurdity only so long as we take the terms
exclusively in their conventional discursive senses. The stumbling
block disappears when we realize that Thoreau has shifted a meaning, has constructed a trope or a play on words. The pun, that highly
compressed form of comparison in which two or more logically dis-
parate meanings are forced to share the same phonemic unit, lends
itself admirably to Thoreau's purpose and underlies many of his
paradoxes, including the example cited above. The peculiar impact
of the paradox lies in our recognition that an expected meaning has
been dislocated by another, remaining within our field of vision but
somewhat out of focus. We are given, in Kenneth Burke's splendid
phrase, a "perspective by incongruity."

The user of paradox thus defines or declares by indirection, frus-
trating "rational" expectations about language. Shortly before the
publication of *Walden,* another New England Transcendentalist, the
theologian Horace Bushnell, affirmed the usefulness of the device,
declaring that "we never come so near to a truly well rounded view
of any truth, as when it is offered paradoxically; that is, under contradictions; that is, when under two or more dictions, which, when
taken as dictions, are contrary to one another." [4] In *Walden,* Thoreau
wants to convey truths of the most unconventional sort—to bring
other minds into proximity and agreement with his own attitudes
and beliefs. He employs paradox not only for its galvanic effect in
persuasion (i.e., as a verbal shock-treatment which reorients the audience), but for the special precision of statement it affords.

At the outset of Thoreau's literary career, his friend Emerson criticized the *"mannerism"* of "A Winter Walk," objecting most strenu-
ously to the oxymorons: "for example, to call a cold place sultry, a
solitude public, a wilderness *domestic.* . . ." [5] And we are not aston-
ished to find that Thoreau himself deprecated the very instrument
he used so skillfully. When he set down in the *Journal* a list of his

4 Horace Bushnell, *God in Christ: Three Discourses* . . . *with a Preliminary Dis-
sertation on Language* (Hartford, 1849), p. 55; cited in Charles Feidelson, Jr., *Symbolism and American Literature* (Chicago, 1953), p. 156.

5 Walter Harding and Carl Bode, eds., *The Correspondence of Henry David
Thoreau* (New York, 1958), p. 137: RWE to HDT, Sept. 18, 1843.

"faults," the first item was "Paradoxes,—saying just the opposite,—a style which may be imitated." [6] On another occasion he complained that a companion, probably Ellery Channing, "tempts me to certain licenses of speech. . . . He asks for a paradox, an eccentric statement, and too often I give it to him." [7] But in spite of these warnings and hesitations (which, incidentally, are echoed in the reservations of some of his most sympathetic later critics), Thoreau did not abandon the paradoxical style. Richard Whately, the author of his college rhetoric text, had acknowledged, though rather reluctantly, the value of the device in argumentation. Thoreau's seventeenth-century reading illustrated its rich literary possibilities. Most important, his ironic sensibility embraced paradox. Thoreau wisely followed what he called the crooked bent of his genius and practiced a rhetoric appropriate to his aims.

These aims were in part determined by the character of Transcendental thinking, with its emphasis upon the perception of a spiritual reality behind the surfaces of things. Nature for the Transcendentalist was an expression of the divine mind; its phenomena, when rightly seen, revealed moral truths. By means of proper perception, said Emerson, "man has access to the entire mind of the Creator," and "is himself the creator" of his own world.[8] The pure, healthy, and self-reliant man, whose mind is in harmony with the Over-Soul, continually discerns the miraculous in the common. But for the timid or degraded man, whose eyes are clouded by convention, nature will appear a "ruin or . . . blank." Idealism is the Transcendentalist's necessary premise: it assures him that things conform to thoughts. By way of demonstration, Emerson tells his uninitiated reader to look through his legs at an inverted landscape. Thoreau was sufficiently tough-minded, and sufficiently interested in the details of natural phenomena, to resist the systematic translation of nature into ideas and moral precepts which Emersonian theory implied. He placed as much emphasis upon the "shams and delusions" which hinder men from "seeing" nature as upon the spiritual meanings of individual natural objects. But he always believed that to recognize one's relations with nature is the basis of moral insight; and he was convinced that the obstacles to this wisdom were removed by the simplification of life. Strip away the artificial, Thoreau tells the "desperate" man, and you will be able to read nature's language. Reality, the "secret of things," lurks under appearances, waiting to be seen. Describing his conversations with the French-Canadian woodchopper, Thoreau says

6 Thoreau, XIII, 7, n.
7 *Ibid.,* XII, 165.
8 *The Complete Works of Ralph Waldo Emerson,* Centenary Edition, 12 vols. (Boston, 1903), I, 64.

he tried to "maneuver" him "to take the spiritual view of things." [9]

The language of *Walden* is, in a very immediate sense, strategic. The problem Thoreau faced there—and to some extent in all his writings—was to create in his audience the "waking moments" in which they could appreciate "the truth of which [he had] been convinced." In other words, he tries to wrench into line with his own the reader's attitudes toward the self, toward society, toward nature, and toward God. He "translates" the reader, raising him out of his conventional frame of reference into a higher one, in which extreme truths become intelligible. To these ends Thoreau employs a rhetoric of powerful exaggeration, antithesis, and incongruity. Habitually aware of the "common sense," the dulled perception that desperate life produces, he could turn the world of his audience upside-down by rhetorical means. He explores new resources of meaning in their "rotten diction" and challenges ingrained habits of thought and action with ennobling alternatives: "Read not the Times," he exhorts in "Life Without Principle." "Read the Eternities." [10] With all the features of his characteristic extravagance—hyperbole, wordplay, paradox, mock-heroics, loaded questions, and the ironic manipulation of cliché, proverb, and allusion—Thoreau urges new perspectives upon his reader. These rhetorical distortions or dislocations, rather than Transcendental doctrines *per se,* are Thoreau's means of waking his neighbors up. They exasperate, provoke, tease, and cajole; they are the chanticleer's call to intellectual morning; they make *Walden,* in the words of John Burroughs, "the most delicious piece of brag in literature." [11]

                                        II

Walden is not, of course, merely a sophisticated sermon. It is the story of an experiment; a narrative; a fable. In 1851, with his "life in the woods" four years behind him and the book which would celebrate that experience, which would give it a permanent artistic and moral focus, still far from finished, Thoreau wrote, "My facts shall be falsehoods to the common sense. I would so state facts that they shall be significant, shall be myths or mythologic." [12] Even the most hortatory sections of the book are grounded in this "mythology" or

9 Thoreau, II, 166.
10 *Ibid.,* IV, 475.
11 Burroughs, "Henry D. Thoreau," *Indoor Studies* (Boston, 1895), p. 29.
12 Thoreau, IX, 99.

significant fiction. I hope to demonstrate that paradox is apposite to the literary design of *Walden:* its themes, symbols, characters, and plot.

As a number of literary theorists have maintained, we can to some extent isolate "a fictional hero with a fictional audience" in any literary work.[13] The "I" of *Walden,* Thoreau as its narrator and hero, is a deliberately created verbal personality. This dramatized Thoreau should not be confused in critical analysis with the surveyor and pencil-maker of Concord: the *persona* stands in the same relation to the man as *Walden*—the symbolic gesture, the imaginative re-creation —stands to the literal fact of the Walden adventure. The narrator is a man of various moods and rhetorical stances, among them the severe moralist, the genial companion, the bemused "hermit," and the whimsical trickster who regards his experiment as a sly joke on solid citizens. The mellowest of all his moods is the one we find, for instance, in "Baker Farm," "Brute Neighbors," and "House-Warming," where he pokes fun at his own zeal as an idealist and reformer. In all his roles he conveys a sense of his uniqueness, the separateness of his vision from that of his townsmen.

The "fictional audience" of *Walden* likewise requires our attention. In defining it I take a hint from Burke, who in "Antony in Behalf of the Play" distinguishes between the play-mob and the spectator-mob as audiences for the oration in *Julius Caesar.* The reader of *Walden,* like Shakespeare's spectator, adopts a double perspective, weighing the speaker's statements both in terms of the fictional circumstance and in terms of their relevance to his own experience. I would distinguish a range of response *within* the dramatic context of *Walden* from an external or critical response. The reader in part projects himself into the role of a hypothetical "listener," whom the narrator addresses directly; and in part he stands at a remove, overhearing this address. Psychologically, we are "beside ourselves in a sane sense," [14] both spectators who respond to *Walden* as an aesthetic entity and vicarious participants in the verbal action. As spectators, or what I will call "readers," we are sympathetic toward the witty and engaging narrator. As projected participants, or what I will term "audience," we must imagine ourselves committed to the prejudices and shortsightedness which the narrator reproves, and subject to the full tone of the address.

---

13 Northrop Frye, *Anatomy of Criticism* (Princeton, 1957), p. 53. See also W. K. Wimsatt, Jr., *The Verbal Icon* (Lexington, Ky., 1954), p. xv; John Crowe Ransom, *The World's Body* (New York, 1938), p. 247ff; René Wellek, "Closing Statement," *Style in Language,* ed. Thomas A. Sebeok (New York, 1960), p. 414.

14 Thoreau, II, 149.

The rhetoric of *Walden,* reflecting in some measure the lecture origins of the early drafts, assumes an initially hostile audience. Thoreau sets up this role for us by characterizing, in the first third of "Economy," a mixed group of silent listeners who are suspicious of the speaking voice. He would address "poor students," "the mass of men who are discontented," and "that seemingly wealthy, but most terribly impoverished class of all, who have accumulated dross." In addition Thoreau creates individual characters who express attitudes to be refuted by the narrator, and who serve as foils for his wit. These are stylized figures, briefly but deftly sketched, who heckle or complain or interrogate. Their function is overtly to articulate the implicit doubts of the audience. "A certain class of unbelievers," "some inveterate cavillers," "housewives . . . and elderly people," "my tailoress," "the hard-featured farmer," "a factory-owner"—such lightly delineated types register their protests against Thoreau's farming techniques, his lack of charity, his conclusions about the pond's depth, his manner of making bread, and even the cleanliness of his bed linen. Their objections tend to be "impertinent," despite Thoreau's disclaimer early in "Economy," to the lower as well as the higher aspects of the experiment. He answers these animadversions with every form of wit: puns, irony, redefinition, paradoxes, twisted proverbs, overstatements, Biblical allusions (cited by a "heathen" to shame the Christian audience), and gymnastic leaps between the figurative and the literal. It is in this context of debate, of challenge and rejoinder, of provocation and rebuttal and exhortation, that the language of *Walden* must be understood. Thoreau's rhetoric is a direct consequence of the way he locates himself as narrator with respect to a hostile fictional audience. The dramatic status of the speaker and his hearers accounts for the extraordinary "audibility" of *Walden* as well as for the aesthetic distance between author and reader.

Our bifurcation into spectator and participant is most intense in the hortatory and satirical passages. In the latter role, we are incredulous, shocked, and subject to the direct persuasive techniques of the argument. As spectator, on the other hand, we applaud Thoreau's rhetorical devastation of the premises of his fictional audience, and, if we find the instructive and polemical statements in *Walden* meaningful, as we most certainly can, we recognize that they are contained by the literary structure, and that they must, as statements about life, be understood first within that context. Even the reader who conforms to the type of the fictional audience, and who brings to *Walden* a full-blown set of prejudices against Thoreauvian "economy," does not stay long to quarrel with the narrator. The force of Thoreau's ridicule encourages him to quit the stage. For the participant, *Walden* is "an invitation to life's dance"; [15] the sympathetic reader dances with Thoreau from the start.

Thoreau's paradoxes are also congenial to the "comic" themes and narrative movement of *Walden*. Using the distinctions of Northrop Frye, we can consider comedy one of the four "mythoi" or recurrent patterns of plot development which may appear in any genre. The "mythos of spring" or comic plot is typified by a rising movement, "from a society controlled by habit, ritual bondage, arbitrary law and the older characters to a society controlled by youths and pragmatic freedom . . . a movement from illusion to reality." [16] Frye's generalization may call to mind a passage in "Conclusion" where Thoreau proclaims the joys of the "awakened" man: "new, universal, and more liberal laws will begin to establish themselves around and within him; or the old laws be expanded, and interpreted in his favor in a more liberal sense, and he will live with the license of a higher order of beings." On the human level, *Walden*'s narrator performs this ascent. On the level of nature, the green life of spring and summer must rise from old winter's bondage, repeating the hero's own movement and prefiguring the spiritual transformation of his audience, "man in the larva state."

Following a traditional comic pattern, Thoreau represents in *Walden* two worlds: the narrator's private paradise and the social wasteland he has abandoned. Each of these polar worlds has its basic character type and body of symbols. The narrator is the *Eiron*, the virtuous or witty character whose actions are directed toward the establishment of an ideal order. The audience and hecklers, who take for granted "what are deemed 'the most sacred laws of society,' " [17] serve as the *Alazon* or impostor. This comic type is a braggart, misanthrope, or other mean-spirited figure, usually an older man, who resists the hero's efforts to establish harmony but who is often welcomed into the ideal order when the hero succeeds. The narrator of *Walden*, both clever and good, withdraws from a society of "skinflint[s]" to a greenwood world at the pond. His pastoral sanctuary is represented in images of moisture, freedom, health, the waking state, fertility, and birth. The society he leaves behind is described in images of dust, imprisonment, disease, blindness, lethargy, and death. Upon these symbolic materials Thoreau builds many of his paradoxes. In his verbal attacks upon the old society, whose "idle and musty virtues" he finds as ridiculous as its vices, the narrator assumes a satirical

---

[15] E. B. White, "Walden—1954," *Yale Review*, XLIV (1954), 13. White does not distinguish between reader and fictional audience.

[16] Frye, p. 169.

[17] Thoreau, II, 355.

or denunciatory pose. When he records his simple *vita nuova*, that is, in the idyllic passages, his tone becomes meditative or ecstatic.

III

But it is, after all, to the dusty world or wasteland that *Walden's* fictional audience belongs. Despite their dissatisfactions, they are committed to this life and its values, and blind to the practical as well as the spiritual advantages of the experiment. The narrator, far from being a misanthropic skulker, wishes to communicate his experience of a more harmonious and noble life. His language serves this end: the first rhetorical function of paradox is to make the audience entertain a crucial doubt. Do they value houses? Thoreau calls them prisons, almshouses, coffins, and family tombs. Farming? It is digging one's own grave. Equipment and livestock? Herds are the keepers of men, not men of herds; and men are "the tools of their tools." Traditional knowledge and a Harvard education? Thoreau describes them as impediments to wisdom. Financial security, or "something [laid up] against a sick day," is the cause of sickness in the man who works for it. Fine and fashionable clothing is a form of decoration more barbaric than tattooing, which is only "skin-deep." The landlord's sumptuous furnishings are really "traps" (an elaborate pun) which hold the holder captive. The railroad, marvel of the industrial age, is a means of transportation ultimately slower than going afoot. Religion, Thoreau tells his pious audience, is a "cursing of God" and distrust of themselves. "Good business," the bulwark of their culture, is the quickest way to the devil. In short, says Thoreau, "the greater part of what my neighbors call good I believe in my soul to be bad, and if I repent of anything, it is very likely to be my good behavior. What demon possessed me that I behaved so well?" These paradoxes, often executed with brilliant humor, jostle and tumble the listener's perspective. To be sure, the narrator is a self-acknowledged eccentric—but he is not a lunatic. Thoreau makes sense in his own terms, and the fictional audience no longer can in theirs.

At the same time as he makes nonsense of the audience's vocabulary with satirical paradoxes, Thoreau appropriates some of its key terms to describe the special values of his life in the woods. For example, though he despises commerce he would conduct a profitable "trade" with the "Celestial Empire." In this second body of rhetorical devices Thoreau again exploits polarities of symbol and idea, and not without irony. But these paradoxes differ sharply in their function from the satirical ones. They attach to the hero's world, to nature and simplified action, the deep connotations of worth which social involvements and material comforts evoke for the desperate man. Thoreau astounds and disarms the audience when he calls his experiment a "business" and renders his accounts to the half- and quarter-penny. By means of this appropriately inappropriate language he announces the incompatibility of his livelihood and his neighbor's, and simultaneously suggests interesting resemblances. Thoreau's enterprise, like the businessman's, requires risks, demands perseverance, and holds out the lure of rewards. The statistical passages of "Economy" and "The Bean-Field" are equivocal. On the one hand, they prove the narrator's ability to beat the thrifty Yankee at his own game; on the other, they parody the Yankee's obsession with finance. Thoreau's argument that a man achieves success in proportion as he reduces his worldly needs is likewise paradoxical, a queer analogue to the commercial theory of increasing profits by lowering costs. He reinforces this unconventional economic principle by declaring that the simple life is to be carefully cultivated and jealously preserved: "Give me the poverty that enjoys true wealth." Similarly he contrasts the rich harvest which a poet reaps from a farm with the *relatively* worthless cash crop, and is eager to acquire the Hollowell place before its owner destroys it with "improvements." I would also include in this category of paradoxes Thoreau's constant reference to fish, berries, and other common natural objects in the language of coins, precious gems, and rare metals; his praise of the humble simpleton as an exalted sage; his assertion that the woods and ponds are religious sanctuaries; and his description of his labors as pastimes and his solitude as companionable. Some related statements carry the mystical overtones of the New Testament: "Not till we are lost, in other words, not till we have lost the world, do we begin to find ourselves." "Walden was dead and is alive again." All these apparent contradictions support Thoreau's triumphant subjectivism in *Walden,* his running proclamation that "The universe constantly and obediently answers to our conceptions." [18] The highest and most sincere conception yields the noblest life.

By nature a dialectical instrument, the paradox is thus stylistically integral to this severely dialectical work. Viewed generally, the two large groups of paradoxes reflect the comic structure of *Walden* and its two major themes: the futility of the desperate life and the rewards of enlightened simplicity. With the paradoxes of the first or satirical group, Thoreau declares that his listener's goods are evils, his freedom slavery, and his life a death. Those of the second group, corresponding rhetorically to the recurrent symbolism of metamorphosis, affirm that the values of the natural and Transcendental life arise from what

[18] *Ibid.,* II, 108.

the audience would deprecate as valueless. In these paradoxes, the beautiful is contained in the ugly, the truly precious in the seemingly trivial, and the springs of life in the apparently dead.

As *Walden* progresses the proportion of the first to the second kind gradually changes. The rhetoric of the early chapters is very largely one of trenchant denunciation, directed against the desperate life. That of the later chapters is predominantly serene, playful, and rapturous. Thoreau creates the impression of a growing concord between himself and his audience by allowing the caustic ironies and repudiations of "Economy" to shift by degrees to the affirmations of "Spring" and "Conclusion." Thoreau the outsider becomes Thoreau the magnanimous insider, around whom reasonable men and those who love life may gather. Rhetorically and thematically, as the book proceeds, the attack becomes the dance.

IV

One of the numerous extended passages in *Walden* which is dominated by oxymoron and which leads itself to close rhetorical analysis is the following, from "Where I Lived, and What I Lived For":

> We do not ride on the railroad; it rides upon us. Did you ever think what those sleepers are that underlie the railroad? Each one is a man, an Irishman, or a Yankee man. The rails are laid on them, and they are covered with sand, and the cars run smoothly over them. They are sound sleepers, I assure you. And every few years a new lot is laid down and run over; so that, if some have the pleasure of riding on a rail, others have the misfortune to be ridden upon. And when they run over a man that is walking in his sleep, a supernumerary sleeper in the wrong position, and wake him up, they suddenly stop the cars, and make a hue and cry about it, as if this were an exception. I am glad to know that it takes a gang of men for every five miles to keep the sleepers down and level in their beds . . . for this is a sign that they may sometime get up again.

In developing his initial paradox and the thesis of the passage, "We do not ride on the railroad; it rides upon us," Thoreau relies heavily upon a pun, for "sleepers" refers simultaneously to the railroad ties and to the benighted laborers who lay them. The repetitions in the short third sentence—"man . . . Irishman . . . Yankee man" —vigorously connect the miserable workers with the more fortunate riders of the cars; they are all in the human family. The train rides on mankind in the sense that a *man* would degrade his life in the railroad enterprise, working on the tracks all day for a pittance. His

life is a form of ˜death; symbolically he has been buried, like the
wooden sleepers which he himself has covered with sand. He may
stay "buried" or "asleep" for many years, perhaps as long as the
wooden ties, the "sound sleepers," remain solid and unrotted. When
Thoreau remarks, "if some have the pleasure of riding on a rail, others
have the misfortune to be ridden upon," he ironically suggests a
brutal insouciance on the part of those wealthy enough to travel over
an extension of the track, laid by new workers. But in terms of the
opening statement, the travelers share the misfortune of being ridden
upon; they are to an extent themselves "sleepers" or unenlightened
men. The occasional sleepwalker struck by the train is very likely
an exhausted laborer, walking on the track in the mental and moral
stupor typical of his way of life. Thoreau calls him a "supernumerary
sleeper," equating once more the literal block of wood with the wooden
man who places it. But "in the wrong position" involves a new paradox: instead of walking stupidly and sleepily on the track—preserving
a merely physical uprightness—he should perhaps have wholly abandoned himself to his futile labor and lain down with the ties. Nevertheless, his calamity excites a "hue and cry." In terms of the railroad's
"economy" he should have been at the same time a sleeper and not a
sleeper. To be struck and run over by the train, or literally to assume
the position of the wooden sleepers in man's last and permanent sleep,
is to be withdrawn from the fruitless life of track-laying, or to be
"awakened." For if the laborer's life is *figuratively* a death and a sleep,
his *actual* death, the end of that existence, would be a birth or a waking. Finally, Thoreau sees in the restlessness of the ties, their tendency
to shift in the roadbed, an intimation that the very workmen who
keep the sleepers down and level may awaken to the dawn of their
own moral day, and rise.

V

The principle of paradox likewise controls individual chapters,
such as "Higher Laws," and fully developed arguments such as the
discussion of philanthropy in the first chapter. It can also be discovered in the juxtaposed rhythms of rise and fall, ascent and descent,
primitivism and transcendence which pervade the imagery and action
of the book. In this last connection we might briefly note that the
Transcendental distinction between what *"is"* and what *"appears to
be"* is reflected in the recurrent contrasting of surface and subsurface
phenomena. When the narrator chases the diving loon, or fishes for
pouts at night, he acts out his pursuit of higher truth. Common sense
will provide only superficial catches; the earnest truth-seeker, the
"hunter and fisher of men," must search beneath appearances and
within himself. The pond in its most consistent symbolic role is the

self, the beholder's own profound nature. Here, as elsewhere, Thoreau ascends by descending: on dark nights his fishing line is lost in the black water below, and his line of thought wanders to "vast and cosmogonal themes in other spheres." The bite of the pout links him to nature again, and as the fish comes wriggling upward, the mind pins down an intuition to a perceived fact. "Thus I caught two fishes as it were with one hook." Legislators prescribe the number of fish-hooks to be permitted at Walden, "but they know nothing about the hook of hooks with which to angle for the pond itself, impaling the legislature for a bait." Thoreau, however, has mastered this fishing lore; he sacrifices social institutions in the quest for himself, for reality. In a similar paradox, Thoreau admits that "Snipes and woodcocks . . . may afford rare sport; but I trust it would be nobler game to shoot one's self."

"Conclusion," which is richer in paradoxes than any other chapter, announces the grand prospects of the awakened life: "In proportion as [a man] simplifies his life, the laws of the universe will appear less complex, and solitude will not be solitude, nor poverty poverty, nor weakness weakness." The chapter reaches its climax in two dramatized paradoxes, fables of metamorphosis. In the first, the timeless artist of Kouroo, like the liberated human spirit Thoreau is celebrating, creates a new and glorious world around himself. The second fable, more humble in its materials but not less marvelous in its import, is the anecdote of a bug which gnaws its way out of an old table, emerging from "society's most trivial and handselled furniture" to enjoy a beautiful and winged life after a long death. "Morning," Thoreau had declared earlier, "is when I am awake and there is a dawn in me." To an audience now capable of sharing his ecsatic vision, his wonder at the infinite possibilities open to the self, he makes his final appeal in the heightened language of paradox: "Only that day dawns to which we are awake. There is more day to dawn. The sun is but a morning star."

The Religion of "Higher Laws"

by John B. Pickard

[Thoreau's] casual disregard of organized religion, his somewhat shocking identification of Christ with Buddha, and his detached estimation of sacred scripture obscure the essential religious cast of his writings. Also his responsiveness to nature's beauty, his intense concern for simplified living, his forceful condemnation of materialism, and his radical struggle against social conformity hide the spiritual nature of his quest in *Walden*. Whereas the student usually studies the more anthologized chapters like "Economy" or "Where I Lived, and What I Lived For," a section like "Higher Laws" is bypassed as being too abstract or philosophical. Yet this chapter contains the quintessence of Thoreau's religious insights and presents a spiritual autobiography in miniature, similar to St. Augustine's *Confessions*. Thoreau's awareness of man's ultimate spirituality and his search for a communion with the divine transcend any formalized religion. "Higher Laws" displays his pure religious impulse, an essential and profoundly moving force that has universal significance.

Of course, the religious sentiment in "Higher Laws" is basically Transcendental. It reflects Emerson's concepts in Nature, that every man possesses an inner spiritual instinct which, if carefully nurtured, will reveal the divine. Though this force may be weakened and coarsened by man's predatory appetite, it can elevate this physical drive and direct it toward a spiritual goal. These fundamental assumptions underlie the entire chapter and are artistically expanded to indicate the paradoxical aspects of man's spiritual search. Unlike the syllogistic approach of the scholastics, Thoreau discusses the nature of spiritual reality with poetic intuition and metaphoric insight. Initially Thoreau defines these laws negatively; they are not the primitive instincts of the wild nor the physical concern for survival. A metaphor of food and eating dominates the chapter to emphasize how these appetites influence man and impel him toward savagery. Being a part of the total man, these natural instincts are good and, if prop-

erly used and disciplined, serve a religious end. At the beginning of
"Higher Laws" Thoreau quietly states that he finds in himself "an
instinct toward a higher, or, as it is named, spiritual life." [1] This instinct differs from the natural instinct, the level of behavior below
reason which dehumanizes man. It is neither the romantic ego, the
following of one's own inner desires, nor an emotional response to
picturesque beauty and physical goodness. This instinct symbolizes
an attraction toward the spiritual existing in all men, which transcends the senses and the individual ego without denying them. Fun-
damentally the chapter is concerned with the complex problem of
reconciling the discordant attractions of the wild (body) and the good
(soul). In a following section this instinct is called a "faint intimation"
which cautions man against consuming animal flesh and fish. For society, catering to its lowest appetites, as represented by its cravings for
mud-turtles and calves' jelly, stultifies the faint, sensitive stirrings of
divine life. These persistent food references repeat the imagistic
motifs of "Economy" where civilization's demand for fashion and deli-
cacies has cooked the soul *à la mode*. Though dim, these intimations
serve as elements of grace, powerful harbingers of the existence of the
divine.

As he proceeds in his definition of higher laws, Thoreau calls them
"poetic faculties," associating them with the imagination, something in-
nate and beyond mere understanding which enables man's mind to
perceive the ultimate supersensuous reality. Finally, in one of the
central passages, Thoreau calls these instincts "the faintest but constant suggestions of his genius" that can never deceive man. Here
"genius" implies neither talent nor the romantic sense of individuality,
but, as Norman Foerster says "the Socratic inner witness," the highest
reality which is the Emersonian concept of self-reliance, the trust in
the inner being through which the Absolute is revealed.[2] No one,
Thoreau triumphantly asserts, was ever misled by his genius, for following it brings about "the true harvest" of man's life. Eventually
these instincts are equated with temperance and chastity—with a rigid
exercise of will and ascetic discipline which transform the brutish and
unclean into direct channels of grace for sainthood. This is the
furthest expanse of Thoreau's imaginative vision, the final fruits of
the seeds of instinct. The chapter stresses the powerful appeal of
opposing natural instincts, which severely tempers his optimistic affirmation that most men can achieve a pure state of blessedness. Through-

---

[1] *The Variorum Walden,* ed. Walter Harding (New York: Twayne Publishers,
Inc., 1962), p. 177. All other quotations, unless otherwise noted, are from the chapter "Higher Laws" in this edition and will not be footnoted.

[2] *Nature in American Literature: Studies in the Modern View of Nature* (N.Y.,
1923), p. 130.

out the chapter Thoreau admits his own impurity and practical failures, expresses his bewilderment at the survival of the animal within, and ultimately determines to practice some new austerity in hopes of redeeming his body.

Just as the full definition of higher laws gradually unfolds, so the chapter organically blends with other sections. Many critics have pointed out that images of renewal and rebirth, of growth and fruition, of daylight and dawn, unify the entire book.[3] Within this chapter a similar metaphoric pattern of growth and change, focusing on the emergence of the good from the wild, occurs. Man's hunter, fisher, trapper activities are a necessary stage in his spiritual evolution and prepare him for the more difficult inner development. Although man is now in the larva stage, ruled by his gross instincts, he should follow the pattern of nature and be transformed into an ethereal butterfly. Highlighting these images of change is the actual location of the chapter within the total seasonal structure of *Walden*. Placed just beyond the central summer chapters which culminate in "The Ponds," its change of emphasis and philosophic tone prepares for the fall and winter chapters where Thoreau builds a chimney for his house, plasters the walls, and lights his November fire. The ascetic discipline extolled in "Higher Laws" prefigures the winter death of Thoreau's sensual nature, the coming cold isolation that permits a religious rebirth, and a return to his vital spiritual core. In a more philosophic manner the chapter illuminates the meaning of the Walden experience. Its abstract tone foreshadows the startling substitution of enclosure (Thoreau's hut) for the expansiveness and freedom of nature; of artificial warmth (his fire) for the sun's natural heat; and of inactivity (thought and meditation) for physical energy. "Higher Laws" also mirrors the preceding water-soul-purity imagery which culminates in "The Ponds." Here Walden Pond, called the lake of light and God's drop, since its purity and serenity exemplify the pristine wonder of God's creation, materially embodies the higher laws. In a transcendent miracle its clear waters physically realize the divine. Now Thoreau questions this vision of "The Ponds" and perceives limitations in his former ecstatic identification of nature with God. For, if the pond contains God, it equally admits the rank and savage which paradoxically destroy the divine. More disturbingly nature keeps alive the predatory instinct in man and satisfies his physical needs along with his spiritual hunger. As Larzer Ziff has indicated, "Higher Laws"

---

[3] Notably Stanley Edgar Hyman, "Henry Thoreau in Our Time," *The Atlantic Monthly*, CLXXVIII (November, 1946), pp. 137-46; R. W. B. Lewis in his *The American Adam: Innocence, Tragedy, and Tradition in the Nineteenth Century* (University of Chicago Press, 1955); Sherman Paul, "Walden: Or, The Metamorphoses," *The Shores of America* (The University of Illinois Press, 1958).

hints at Thoreau's eventual disenchantment with nature's mystic intuitions, where bafflement and frustration with a nature that encourages the sensual in man replace his early raptures.[4] If the wild obscured the meaning of the higher laws, and the primitive aspects of life could no longer be equally reverenced with the good, then a withdrawal from Walden was necessary. Nature fails to reveal the divine in a pantheistic sense and even its transcendental power can be doubted. "Higher Laws" moves Thoreau much more closely to a Puritan withdrawal from nature and a distrust of the senses, where continence becomes the prime virtue and sexuality is sublimated to chastity. Rebirth occurs only if nature is overcome and the mind and spirit fully cultivated. In a sense the chapter suggests that the ideal can never be realized in nature and that society and civilization are more suitable to spiritual renewal. The tone of the chapter clearly indicates that the Walden experience is behind him and from this vantage point Thoreau notes: "If I were to live in a wilderness I should again be tempted to become a fisher and hunter in earnest."

Though "Higher Laws" outlines Thoreau's religious feelings he dramatizes these abstractions by suggestive, vivid metaphors, Biblical and mythical allusions, and short fables. Nowhere is his gift for original metaphor better displayed than in the chapter's opening. Coming home one evening with a string of fish, Thoreau sees a woodchuck and experiences "a strange thrill of savage delight, and was strongly tempted to seize and devour him raw." This disturbing image conveys the full paradox of Thoreau's relationship with nature where the violent rush of natural appetite lays bare the predatory creature hidden beneath nature's beneficent surface. Wonderingly Thoreau recollects that at times he had found himself "ranging the woods, like a half-starved hound," that he had eaten fried rat with relish, and that he could still be a hunter "in earnest." Although these acts make life bestial and seemingly deny the spiritual instinct, they must be reverenced. They contain the primary basis of life in which the divine principles are waiting to be illuminated by denial and purification. In another passage, still bothered by these conflicting instincts and by the persistent survival of the brutish, Thoreau remembers finding "the lower jaw of a hog, with white and sound teeth and tusks, which suggested that there was an animal health and vigor distinct from the spiritual." Here the color white, previously applied to the holiness of the higher laws and the purity of Walden Pond, is found in an animal most associated with filth and gluttony. From the rankest corruption and decay emerge soundness and physical purity, mocking man's attempts to achieve chastity by temperance and discipline. Like the

[4] *Walden: A Writer's Edition* (New York: Holt, Rinehart and Winston, Inc., 1961), p. 313.

metaphor of the woodchuck, this image explores the ambivalent relationship of the wild and the good, of the sensuous and the higher
laws. By Transcendental theory these two instincts should supple-
ment each other, but in actual experience they contradict one another.
It is little wonder that Thoreau is haunted by these images for they
bring into question the whole meaning of his Walden experience and
force him to qualify his optimistic vision of man's harmony with
nature.

Another technique employed in this chapter is the creative development of Biblical associations to underscore the religious nature of the
higher laws. The chapter's main metaphor is an elaborate expansion
of Christ's demand that His Apostles be fishers of men, catching the
spiritual rather than the physical. As the chapter opens with Thoreau
carrying fish, so the remainder meditates on the nature of fishing, its
values, and its relationship to man's inner life. Fishing and hunting
bring a youth into close contact with nature, develop his aesthetic
responses, and sharpen his perceptions and senses. This continual
contact with nature is youth's first step toward manhood, since the
physical acts of hunting and fishing prefigure his maturity as a
"mighty" hunter after a game not found "in this or any vegetable
wilderness." Using the early Christian significance of the fish image,
Thoreau equates fishers and hunters with holy men and finds a religious meaning in their actions. The Biblical associations of hunters
in Genesis echo these remarks. The hunter and first-born Esau, the
wanderer and lover of the wild, later loses his birthright to his
brother Jacob who significantly does not hunt but toils as a farmer,
an occupation better suited to the more advanced stage of civilization.

As this passage progresses Thoreau expands images of change and
evolution, calling hunting a "stage," an "introduction," and even
"the most original part" of man, since it is one of man's earliest
meaningful acts. These activities are described as seeds which must
be planted in the physical to produce an entirely different flower
and fruit. Only "at first" or in the initial stages of his spiritual learning process should the youth be an actual hunter, for full manhood
depends upon the youth's ability to distinguish and follow his "last"
or ultimate goal. Still Thoreau sadly observes that "the mass of men
are still and always young in this respect." This phrase consciously
reiterates his bitter denunciation of the desperate lives of the mass
of men in "Economy" who are brutalized by ceaseless work and concern for luxuries. Materially oriented clergymen fare even worse.
Thoreau dismisses them as good shepherd's dogs, since their lives
make such a mockery of Christ's example seen in the parable of the
Good Shepherd. Finally, Thoreau widens his fishing-hunting metaphor
to include legislators who have allowed civilized trivia to obscure

their original nature. Although the legislators make the economic and social laws that govern men, they ironically overlook the spiritual laws upon which theirs are based. While legislating on the physical size of hooks for fishing, they neglect man's spiritual insight, the "hook of hooks," which would enable them to angle for the very meaning of life ("the pond itself"). Instead of being fishermen, Thoreau concludes, they remain mere bait.

The fable of John Farmer which closes the chapter demonstrates Thoreau's ability artistically to express his religious feelings. With poetic intensity he restates the essential religious meaning of his *Walden* experience, that man is both natural and divine and that he must discover the spiritual laws which are a part of nature and yet beyond it. Although Thoreau tries to reconcile the conflicts of the good and the wild, he concludes, as does the chapter, by stressing the need for conscious discipline and chastity to redeem the natural appetites. The fable opens:

> John Farmer sat at his door one September evening, after a hard day's work, his mind still running on his labor more or less. Having bathed he sat down to recreate his intellectual man. It was a rather cool evening, and some of his neighbors were apprehending a frost. He had not attended to the train of his thoughts long when he heard some one playing on a flute, and that sound harmonized with his mood.

The folk hero of the fable, John Farmer, is, of course, an everyman, but he is also a farmer working closely with nature and instinctively responsive to nature's spiritual significance. However, he fails to be "Man on the farm," as Emerson envisioned him in *The American Scholar,* for his special farm vocation has obscured the total man. Significantly John Farmer sits on his doorstep—on the threshold—a part of a definite framework (his house and society) and also a gateway to nature. With this action he has prepared himself for the faint intimations of the higher law. After the hard physical work of the day, he has bathed and washed off the dirt of the fields, the aspect of the wild that coarsens and may brutalize the intellectual man. Since the pond and water have been associated with rebirth and purity throughout *Walden,* this act symbolizes an inner baptism and spiritual readiness as well. Only with the completion of this ritual can John Farmer begin his transformation to "Man on the farm." It is a cool September evening, the beginning of the fall and winter season, directly foreshadowed by the mention of frost. Following the fall's harvest, the winter season brings enclosure, isolation, and ultimately spiritual renewal. It comes as a cold dark evening after a day of physical activity and growth under the warm summer sun. John Farmer is now

ready to retire within himself, to endure a temporary death of the
senses in order to discover spiritual reality.

He finds his mind immeshed in the temporal, physical activities of
the day. The verb "running" suggests the dominating force of the
physical, the difficulty of ceasing sensual movement and material in-
volvement to permit spiritual control. Unlike his neighbors, the mass
of men, John Farmer is not apprehensive about the coming frost, for
he sees beyond its economic danger to its spiritual significance. While
he sits, unwillingly plotting future labors, the music of a flute sounds
and under its magic spell he envisions a new kind of work far beyond
his farmer's vocation. As an instrument of Pan, the half-man, half-
beast demigod, the flute aptly symbolizes man's gradual, though incomplete, emergence to divinity. The flute's beautiful tones indicate
the spiritual riches available to those who properly listen. Its sounds
are the vibrations of the Aeolian harp, the music of the spheres
whose harmony initiates man into the mysteries of the higher laws.
Though John Farmer has properly placed himself at his door and
washed, this mystical music begins when he is partially engrossed in
his day's activities. Beauty and spiritual insight are not divorced from
the mundane, nor are they obtained by conscious effort. Under the in-
cantation of the music John Farmer realizes that the material products
of his labor and his mental planning are only preparatory, "the scurf
of his skin." They merely indicate the "work for certain faculties
which slumbered in him." As he responds more fully to the music,
time and space are transcended, for the notes do away with "the
street, the village, and the state in which he lived." He departs from
the physical state, the actual state and country where he lives, the
vocational state of his farmer's existence, and his individual mental
state, to find a new glorious one of blessedness. In the midst of his
vision, he wonders how he is to leave his present "mean, moiling life"
and migrate toward the ideal.

Since no formula exists for a mystical experience, no explicit answer
is given. Rather, Thoreau indicates that John Farmer must pursue
his farming, for the flute's tonal vision cannot be permanently grasped
nor even readily duplicated again. He must return to his labor and
through it seek the higher laws. Thoreau ends the fable: "All he could
think of was to practise some new austerity, to let his mind descend
into his body and redeem it, and treat himself with ever increasing
respect." These three clauses draw together the whole chapter, while
echoing the central phrases of the book, "Simplicity, simplicity, simplicity." First John Farmer must exercise a stricter spiritual economy
to integrate his vision with actual life. The next clause examines how
this is to be done. Redemption or a state of blessedness results from a
close working with the material at hand instead of a romantic pursuit

of a distant music. As an extension of the higher law, the mind must descend and redeem the body, transmuting the "grossest sensuality into purity and devotion." The evident religious implications of Christ's incarnation and redemption of mankind in "descent" and "redeem" serve here as an eternal emblem of ultimate rebirth. Finally and simply John Farmer is to treat himself with respect, since his body has been described as a "temple," the exterior form which shelters the divine. Austerity, redemption, and respect are all united in the actual work of farming, for the higher law depends on and exists in the actual. As the fable opened with John Farmer both in his house and nature, so it closes with his return to work in an attempt to harmonize the physical and the spiritual.

In "Higher Laws" Thoreau's religious insight is expressed at its most complex and dramatic. He explores the paradox of how the wild and good can be fused in a larger moral scheme, expresses his personal doubts about nature's embodiment of the divine, and finally counsels actual subjection of nature by temperance and purity. Through ascetic discipline man can hear the faint intimations of the spirit and respond to the principles of the higher law to realize his divine potential. Purposefully undogmatic and limited by no sectarian creed, "Higher Laws" contains the essentials of all religious experience and affirms the validity of man's spiritual quest.

Ancient Rites at Walden

by Reginald L. Cook

"In the mythus a superhuman intelligence uses the unconscious thoughts and dreams of men as its hieroglyphics to address men unborn." Henry Thoreau: *A Week on the Concord and Merrimack Rivers.*

A key thinker in the Transcendental movement—and a deeply religious one—is Henry Thoreau. His master work, *Walden,* is a seminal book for several reasons, among which, first and foremost, must always be what it reflects implicitly and explicitly, not only of the Christian tradition, but of other ancient traditions, especially the Greek. It is the purpose of this paper to indicate correlations between the New England Transcendentalist and some of the myths from other ancient traditions. Here, in *Walden,* are myths which lie a little below the surface and re-enforce our belief that at times consciously and, at other times instinctively, Thoreau drew upon these rich sources giving his master work an extra-Christian dimension. The myths add allusiveness, metaphor, story, and idea to his narrative; above all, they complement the activating "traditional Christian elements" often noted in general and specific commentaries.

"Great things in literature, Greek plays for example," writes Jane Harrison, "I most enjoy when behind their bright splendours I see moving darker and older shapes." A first reading of Walden does not commonly turn to light the darker and older shapes, but most readers see the "bright splendours." Later, dark shapes are seen moving distinctly beneath the surface. Such awareness is no new thing. Of the ritual and mythology that once visibly guided man's conscious life, Heinrich Zimmer says: "The spiritual heritage of archaic man has vanished to a large extent from the surface of the tangible and conscious realm, yet survives and remains ever present in the subterranean layers of the unconscious." So it does in *Walden.* Both consciously and instinctively Thoreau reacted to "the subterranean layers of the unconscious," and traces of a deeply embedded inheritance are

recognized in the play of the darker and older shapes which give
Walden a peculiarly original meaning. Although it was not Thoreau's
conscious intent to re-enact a myth, nevertheless *Walden* is a complete, dynamic, and symbolic narrative. The sojourn of two years and
two months at the Pond represents a ritualistic cycle, and Thoreau's
theories, sanctioned pragmatically as deeds, have a counterpart in
sacramental observances. Even the form (the progression of the
seasons) is one with the meaning (the regeneration of the human
spirit).

Since Thoreau was effectively cross-fertilized by foreign cultures,
Walden fairly teems with allusions to and quotations from the classic
sources of Hindu, Greek, and Roman myth, of Chinese sacred writings and the great English tradition, and even of native history where
the past survives in protean forms. His affinity for mythology is apparent. Mary Hosmer Brown writes in *Memories of Concord:* "Aunt
Jane said that Thoreau and her father discussed Scandinavian mythology so much that she became an adept in those legends. Such a
deep impression was made on her mind that in later life she was
compelled to translate Greek and Roman myths back into her early
models of Thor, Woden, and Igdrasil." In *Walden* Thoreau refers
to the Parcae and Momus, to the Hesperides and the Etesian winds,
to the Herculean labors and the gods of Troy. He identifies with
Antaeus; he associates Olympus with the outside of the earth everywhere, and bullfrogs with a local Stygian lake. He sacrifices an old
forest fence to Vulcan, and sees a resemblance between the stacked
ice cakes on Walden Pond and "a vast blue fort or Valhalla." Acheron,
Aurora, Hygeia, and Hebe are his familiars. When he does not refer
directly to a myth, as in a pack of hounds pursuing their Actaeon, he
implies an association. The railroad engine is a Homeric cloud-
compeller, and the classics of literature resemble a pile by which he
may scale heaven at last, like the Titans piling Pelion on Ossa to
reach the stronghold of the gods.

A more searching look discloses ritual forms of purgation and sacrifice, formulas of prayer, a quest, or an ordeal, but whatever form they
take their re-enactment enlightens the mysteries of ritual consciously
or unconsciously performed. "In dealing with symbols and myths from
far away we are really conversing somehow with ourselves—with a
part of ourselves, however, which is as unfamiliar to our conscious
being as the interior of the earth to the students of geology," says
Heinrich Zimmer. "Hence the mythical tradition provides us with a
sort of map for exploring and ascertaining contents of our own inner
being to which we consciously feel only scantily related." A man's
behavior reflects importantly on the direction of his destiny. *Walden*
is not remarkable as a repository of magical tokens like Cuchullin's

magic belt, Owain's ring, or Faust's magic key. It is rather the narrative of the epiphanies Thoreau makes while journeying along a secular trail. It is, in effect, an initiatory quest—an ordeal by self-exile from Concord village—and the ritualistic period of testing evokes Wordsworthian "far-off things," none of which are remotely associated with knightly tourneys, medieval amour, fair isles, or enchanted castles.

The 'traditional ghosts' (Jane Harrison's phrase) which appear apparitionlike have no association with aggressive images of dragon-slayers like Siegfried, Tristan, Indra, or Owain of the Round Table. Theseus killed the Minotaur. Perseus slew the sea-monster. Hercules fought the Hydra. But no such symbolic parallelism runs through Walden. What was once hostile and incomprehensible in nature is now domesticated, without sacrificing wonder or gaiety. Although science and rationalism have diminished the terror in nature, we have not lost the grace of wonder *within* nature. Like his contemporaries, Thoreau was stirred by the natural scene. "I cannot spare water or wine/Tobacco-leaf or poppy or rose," says Emerson. "Let me feel thee again, old sea! Let me leap into thy saddle once more," exclaims Melville. "I believe a leaf of grass is no less than the journey-work of the stars," asserts Whitman. Similarly, Thoreau is prepared to see the strange and unusual in a familiar landscape. "When I crossed Flint's Pond, after it was covered with snow, though I had often paddled about and skated over it, it was so unexpectedly wide and so strange that I could think of nothing but Baffin's Bay."

The magic which man exercises by tools, weapons, agriculture, metallurgy, domestic craft, and with the arts does concern Thoreau, and in some of this magic—notably in agriculture and the arts—he is adept. But, in the main, we shall have to look elsewhere for the key symbolic image which identifies him with Freud's conception of myth as "the secular dream of the race." The key is to be found in the means he chose in his quest; not in escape from but confrontation of experience. Thoreau thought a man should have a clear sense of his objectives, or the exactions of society would impose devitalizing tasks upon him. In effect, he must learn how to manage his own affairs. Let him first learn how to take care of himself. When read from this point of vantage *Walden* illustrates the inward operations of the spirit. On one level, *Walden* is the record of an economic experiment whose objective is self-sufficiency. On a complementary level, it is a moral poem which embodies self-reformation. Pragmatically, both experiments succeeded. Thoreau found by living the life he imagined, he could free himself from social conformity and activate a state of mind where new, universal, and more liberal laws were established around and within him, which is to say, he discovered he could unite harmoniously the conscious and the unconscious forces of life. By living a life of "voluntary poverty," he solved his economic problems and by enjoying "a wide halo of ease and leisure," he was free to tap the deeper instinctual forces. One of the lessons he learned is that identity is realized in process rather than in fixity. "I left the woods for as good a reason as I went there. Perhaps it seemed to me that I had several more lives to live, and could not spare any more time for that one."

Before he left 'the woods,' in his quest to live 'sturdily and Spartan-like,' he had submitted to a poetic self-exile. *Walden* re-enacts the initiation and the tests in the ordeal which accompanied the quest. In the chapters on "Economy," "The Bean-field," and "House-Warming," we learn how he met the test of survival. The test of solitariness is described in "Solitude," of fellowship in "Visitors," of intellectual challenge in "Reading," of moral reformation in "Higher Laws." The account in *Walden* fairly burgeons with ceremonial gestures such as bathing, hoeing, building, and even in his tutelary concern for the red huckleberry, sand cherry, red pine, black ash, white grape, yellow violet, and nettle tree. His hospitality had a ritualistic confirmation in the tribal custom of the Indians. Sacramental moments were celebrated by his practise of an ancient purification ritual. "Every morning was a cheerful invitation to make my life of equal simplicity, and I may say innocence, with Nature herself. I have been as sincere a worshipper of Aurora as the Greeks. I got up early and bathed in the pond; that was my religious exercise, and one of the best things which I did." This daily ritual associates him with the native gods and mythical ancestors who perform their sacramental rites in a stoup of lustral water. His idealistic talismans are hound, bay horse, and turtledove, for which he searches with the ardent hopefulness of Novalis and "the blue flower." His totem is the ground-nut (*Apios tuberosa*), "a sort of fabulous fruit," and the potato of the aborigines. His magic balm is the colorless water of the pond, which, when held up to the light in a glass, is "as colorless as an equal quantity of air" and "of such crystalline purity that the body of the bather appears of an alabaster whiteness." His magic balm is comparable to the Greek Ambrosia and Vedic "Amrita." "I am thankful that this pond was made deep and pure as a symbol," he says.

The culmination of the tests appears in "Spring" with purgation, rebirth, and regeneration. His purgation is symbolized by the frost coming out of the ground. In his startlingly imaginative analogue, he sees the pattern of nature flowing organically with the spring thaw—a pattern that reminds him of the prototypic leaf, of the formation of blood-veins, of the source of rivers, of the bony system, of the fleshy fibre, and cellular tissue. The thaw is the pressure from within. "It precedes the green and flowery spring, as mythology precedes regular poetry." Just as Walden was dead but is alive again, so does he also feel the re-enactment of rebirth and regeneration. The symbol is the spring grass flaming on the hillside "like a spring fire." With measured conviction he says, "So our human life but dies down to its root, and still puts forth its green blade to eternity." Of all the sacramental rituals which *Walden* embodies, none is more revelatory and essential in understanding Thoreau than the purgation-regeneration ritual. What it signifies is self-transcendence through self-purification; not by rejecting the society of man does he seek the higher laws but by self-reformation.

In *The King and the Corpse,* Heinrich Zimmer tells us that "archaic man regarded himself as a part of the animal world of nature and identified himself with the traits and powers of the more impressive among his surrounding animal neighbors." *Walden* invites a parallelism between Thoreau's *rapport* with the creatures of the field, stream, and woodland stand *and* archaic man. In "Higher Laws" he refers to his youthful instinct to kill the creatures of the woods. In his later years the instinct is no longer assertive. This change in attitude is paralleled in history. A process of humanization took place in medieval times through the influence of the Christian faith and the chivalric ideal. Of the young man, Thoreau says: "He goes thither at first as a hunter and fisher, until at last, if he has the seeds of a better life in him, he distinguishes his proper objects, as a poet or naturalist it may be, and leaves the gun and fish-pole behind." Or, as Zimmer interprets the post-medieval view: "Not of killing the animal soul inside and setting ourselves apart from it (like Hercules in Greek myth who killed the lion of Nemea and wore its flayed skin as symbolic of the domination of the whole animal Kingdom), but of converting the beast to the human cause—winning it over, so that it should be as helpmate in the great and difficult task of forging a union between the human and extra-human powers that inhabit not the cosmos only but also ourselves."

The 'winning over' appears in Thoreau's intimate *rapport* with loon and woodchuck, squirrel and partridge, ant and owl. Not to the degree that the creatures of the extra-human kingdom become helpmates as the lion served the necessities of Owain in his perilous questing or Hercules in his conquest of the king of the animal world, but as our familiar. The local rabbits and partridges represented "ancient and venerable families known to antiquity as to modern times; of the very hue and substance of Nature, nearest allied to leaves and to the ground. . . ." The partridges were his "hens and chickens." On occasion he watched a barred owl for a half hour on a winter day until he felt "a slumbrous influence." In the great background of mythology the owl is the oracular bird, the voice of the wilderness untouched by human culture. It possesses the secrets of the forest. Listening to the screech-and-hoot owls Thoreau drew closer to the dark, demonic nocturnal forces which also operate in nature. "All day the sun has shone on the surface of some savage swamp—but now a more dismal and fitting day dawns, and a different race of creatures awakes to express the meaning of Nature there." Not only does *Walden* renew the primitive custom in the present, it also reflects the naturalization of primitive forces. "It is hardly as if you had seen a wild creature when a rabbit or a partridge bursts away," he says significantly, "only a natural one, as much to be expected as rustling leaves." What is neither naturalized nor domesticated—like the barred owl, for instance—is recognized for what it is. The dragons and sea-monsters and hydras are gone, but these other creatures—the partridge chicks, squirrels, loons, and woodchucks—survive, like us, as remnants of ancient tribes.

There are *at least* two *Waldens*. One is the homely, circumstantial, and actual record; the other is ancient, ritualistic, and hieratic. In *Meditations on Quixote*, Gasset reminds us "for the Greeks, only the earliest things are fully poetic, not because they are old but because they are the oldest, because they contain in themselves the foundation and the causes. The stock of myths which made up at the same time the traditional religion, physics, and history contains all the poetic material of Greek art in its best period. The poet has to start from it, and moves within it, although it may be to alter it, as the tragic poets do." It is this old world which Thoreau, a good Greek if a better Brahmin, inhabited. How poetic the association is remains to be seen. The poetry is in the feeling that the ancient images of myths flickering on the wall of the present evoked in his imagination. As a poetic labor, the images of the present—the pond, the woodlot, the bean-field, Brister's spring, Fair Haven hill, Goose Pond, the village—represent the external reality, but he was always aware of another reality—a Greek reality, which Gasset describes as "the essential, the profound and latent; not the external appearance but the living sources of all appearance." Emerson was aware of this reality, and in "Fate," he warned: "We cannot trifle with this reality, this outcropping in our planted gardens of the core of the world." In a sense, it is true the spiritual reality to which Emerson refers and the archetypal reality of the ideal to which Gasset refers are one and the same. The poetry is evoked by what the veiled appearance suggests of the ancient essential reality. The Iron Horse introduces Thoreau to a "new mythology"; it has this significance. But when he is making bread he is directly associated with a primitive act that relates him to an ancient essential reality. So "the arching and sheaf-like top of the wool-grass" becomes an archetypal fact. It "brings back the summer to (Thoreau's) winter memories." It stands in his mind as "an antique style, *older than Greek or Egyptian.*" (My italics.) Our world of eternal reality is indeed only a delicately veiled appearance.

The theme of the reactualization of the archetypal gestures of archaic man—the gestures of baptism and planting and harvesting, or curative ceremonials and re-birth—and their ritualistic evidences appear as naturally as the pickerel in the pond. The more searchingly *Walden* is read with Jane Harrison's statement concerning "the darker and older shapes" in mind the more various the shapes appear. In "Economy" Thoreau writes drily: "In Arcadia, when I was there, I did not see any hammering stone." Laconic as it is, this satiric reference hints of a wider context. The point of Thoreau's satiric thrust is the pretension of builders—especially the pretension of emperors, satraps, and princes of old whose lust for ostentatious luxury expressed itself in towers and temples of unexampled grandeur. Not only an individual but a people, a nation, is often excessively concerned with perpetuating its memory by "hammered stone"—a monument, a pyramid, a catafalque, a temple, a row of statues. All this grandiosity was vulgar to Thoreau, who loved better to see stones, as he said, "in place." To an imaginative Transcendentalist and a passionate devotee of his own Concord ambient, Arcadia would be the right place to cite in contrast to Thebes, Memphis, or Rome.

In his allusion Thoreau is following not in the lead of the Greeks in their unidealized description of Arcadia but the Latin poets—especially Virgil—who stressed the ideal loveliness of Arcadia. Arcadia evokes in his imagination a picture of a Utopian homeland where simple piety prevails, and where the rustic amenities of life are experienced without either lavishness or grandiosity. Forevermore it glimmers on the Thoreauvian romantic horizon as a Virgilian place of bucolic charm where shepherds and sylvan dieties dance, and sing, and love. It is exactly the place for a man who had travelled much in Concord to indulge his solitariness. No one, apparently, was any more lonely in Arcadia than "a single mullein or dandelion in a pasture, or a bean leaf, a sorrel, or a horsefly, or a bumblebee." There you could exercise your exuberance with impunity. You did not at least spend any time in such an extravagant way as lavish living and luxuriant accommodations would imply. You hammered stone; you lived it up on beans and rice.

Similarly, passage after passage in *Walden,* whether referring to sacred fire, or time, or gardening, or whatever, evokes "darker and older shapes" whose significance grips the imagination because they are so much a part of our pre-historical as well as our historical past. Interpreted in this light these passages complement and re-enforce an extra-Christian dimension in *Walden*. It can then be read on two levels most rewardingly to the imaginative reader. There is the level of the dramatic present and the level of the pre-historic past. It is not the conscious level of the "new mythology" of the Iron Horse with which we are here primarily concerned, but the "memory" of the "elderly dame," to whom Thoreau refers in "Solitude," who dwelt in his neighborhood and in whose odorous herb-garden he loved to stroll sometimes, "gathering simples and listening to her fables." It is this old dame—*Alma natura*—who could tell, as he says with neat whimsicality, "the original of every fable, and on what fact every one is founded, for the incidents occurred when she was young." For the most part the incidents did occur when she was young. We also get glimpses into ourselves. Although our atavisms are commonly refined away by the educative process, we are haunted by an unknown past or, as Dr. Jung says, by "a collective unconscious." What the enchanted herb was to Medea the Walden experience was to Thoreau. This is what is meant when *Walden* is referred to as a complete, dynamic, and symbolic narrative. The total experience—the conscious and instinctual re-enactment of rituals and the multiple epiphanies which illuminate Thoreau's journeying along a secular trail—is the substance of *Walden*. The experience is the pill to which he refers in a passage at the close of "Solitude" and which kept him well. It is the pill of his "greatgrandmother Nature's universal vegetable, botanic medicine." He was not a worshipper of Hygeia but rather of Hebe, "cupbearer to Jupiter," who had the power of restoring gods and men to the vigor of youth.

Transcendental Pastoral[1]

by Leo Marx

Walden . . . may be read as the report of an experiment in transcendental pastoralism. The organizing design is like that of many American fables: *Walden* begins with the hero's withdrawal from society in the direction of nature. The main portion of the book is given over to a yearlong trial of Emerson's prescription for achieving a new life. When Thoreau tells of his return to Concord, in the end, he seems to have satisfied himself about the efficacy of this method of redemption. It may be difficult to say exactly what is being claimed, but the triumphant tone of the concluding chapters leaves little doubt that he is announcing positive results. His most telling piece of evidence is *Walden*—the book itself. Recognizing the clarity, coherence, and power of the writing, we can only conclude—or so transcendental doctrine would have it—that the experiment has been a success. The vision of unity that had made the aesthetic order of *Walden* possible had in turn been made possible by the retreat to the pond. The pastoral impulse somehow had provided access to the order latent in the cosmos.

But the meaning of *Walden* is more complicated than this affirmation. Because Thoreau takes seriously what Emerson calls the "method of nature"—more seriously than the master himself—the book has a strong contrapuntal theme. Assuming that natural facts properly perceived and accurately transcribed must yield the truth, Thoreau adopts the tone of a hard-headed empiricist. At the outset he makes it clear that he will tell exactly what happened. He claims to have a craving for reality (be it life or death), and he would have us believe him capable of reporting the negative evidence. Again and again he allows the facts to play against his desire, so that his prose at its best acquires a distinctively firm, cross-grained texture. Though the dominant one is affirmative, the undertone is skeptical, and it qualifies the import of episode after episode. For this reason *Walden* belongs

1 Title supplied by the editor.
From The Machine in the Garden: Technology and the Pastoral Ideal in America, *by Leo Marx. Copyright © 1964 by Oxford University Press, Inc. Reprinted by permission of the publisher.*

among the first in a long series of American books which, taken together, have had the effect of circumscribing the pastoral hope, much as Virgil circumscribes it in his eclogues. In form and feeling, indeed, Thoreau's book has much in common with the classic Virgilian mode.

Although the evidence is abundant, it is easy to miss the conventional aspect of *Walden*. In the second chapter Thoreau describes the site as an ideal pasture, a real place which he transforms into an unbounded, timeless landscape of the mind. And he identifies himself with Damodara (Krishna) in his rôle as shepherd, and with a shepherd in a Jacobean song:

> There was a shepherd that did live,
> And held his thoughts as high
> As were the mounts whereon his flocks
> Did hourly feed him by.

Nevertheless, the serious affinity between *Walden* and the convention is disguised by certain peculiarities of American pastoralism, the most obvious being the literalness with which Thoreau approaches the ideal of the simple life. For centuries writers working in the mode had been playing with the theme, suggesting that men might enrich their contemplative experience by simplifying their housekeeping. (The shepherd's ability to reduce his material needs to a minimum had been one of his endearing traits.) Yet it generally had been assumed that the simple life was a poetic theme, not to be confused with the way poets did in fact live. In the main, writers who took the felicity of shepherds in green pastures as their subject had been careful to situate themselves near wealth and power. The effect of the American environment, however, was to break down common-sense distinctions between art and life. No one understood this more clearly than Henry Thoreau; skilled in the national art of disguising art, in *Walden* he succeeds in obscuring the traditional, literary character of the pastoral withdrawal. Instead of writing about it—or *merely* writing about it— he tries it. By telling his tale in the first person, he endows the mode with a credibility it had seldom, if ever, possessed. Because the "I" who addresses us in *Walden* is describing the way he had lived, taking pains to supply plenty of hard facts ("Yes, I did eat $8.74, all told. . . ."), we scarcely notice that all the while he had been playing the shepherd's venerable rôle. He refuses to say whether the book is an explicit guide for living or an exercise in imaginative perception. We are invited to take it as either or both. Convinced that effective symbols can be derived only from natural facts, Thoreau had moved to the pond so that he might make a symbol of his life. If we miss the affinity with the Virgilian mode, then, it is partly because we are dealing with a distinctively American version of romantic pastoral.

No feature of *Walden* makes this truth more apparent than its topography. The seemingly realistic setting may not be a land of fantasy like Arcadia, yet neither is it Massachusetts. On inspection it proves to be another embodiment of the American moral geography— a native blend of myth and reality. The hut beside the pond stands at the center of a symbolic landscape in which the village of Concord appears on one side and a vast reach of unmodified nature on the other. As if no organized society existed to the west, the mysterious, untrammeled, primal world seems to begin at the village limits. As in most American fables, the wilderness is an indispensable feature of this terrain, and the hero's initial recoil from everyday life carries him to the verge of anarchic primitivism.[2] "We need the tonic of wildness," Thoreau explains, using the word "pasture" to encompass wild nature: "We need to witness our own limits transgressed, and some life pasturing freely where we never wander." (The combined influence of geography and the romantic idea of nature—sublime Nature—gives rise to attitudes held by a long line of American literary heroes from Natty Bumppo to Ike McCaslin.) But Thoreau is not a primitivist. True, he implies that he would have no difficulty choosing between Concord and the wilderness. What really engages him, however, is the possibility of avoiding that choice. (Jefferson had taken the same position.) In *Walden*, accordingly, he keeps our attention focused upon the middle ground where he builds a house, raises beans, reads the *Iliad*, and searches the depths of the pond. Like the "navel of the earth" in the archaic myths studied by Mircea Eliade, the pond is the absolute center—the *axis mundi*—of Thoreau's cosmos. If an alternative to the ways of Concord is to be found anywhere, it will be found on the shore of Walden Pond—near the mystic center.

And it had best be found quickly. The drama of *Walden* is intensified by Thoreau's acute sense of having been born in the nick of time. Though the book resembles the classic pastoral in form and feeling, its facts and images are drawn from the circumstances of life in nineteenth-century America. By 1845, according to Thoreau, a depressing state of mind—he calls it "quiet desperation"—has seized the people of Concord. The opening chapter, "Economy," is a diagnosis of this cultural malady. Resigned to a pointless, dull, routinized existence,

---

2 The difference between the typical American hero and the shepherd in traditional versions of pastoral is suggested by Renato Poggioli's account of that archetypal figure as one who "lives a sedentary life even in the open, since he prefers to linger in a grove's shade rather than to wander in the woods. He never confronts the true wild, and this is why he never becomes even a part-time hunter." Given the circumstances of American life, our heroes do confront the true wild, and they often become hunters. But it is striking to notice how often they are impelled to restrict or even renounce their hunting. I am thinking of Natty Bumppo, Melville's Ishmael, Faulkner's Ike McCaslin, and Thoreau himself.

Thoreau's fellow-townsmen perform the daily round without joy or anger or genuine exercise of will. As if their minds were mirrors, able only to reflect the external world, they are satisfied to cope with things as they are. In Emerson's language, they live wholly on the plane of the Understanding. Rather than design houses to fulfill the purpose of their lives, they accommodate their lives to the standard design of houses. Thoreau discovers the same pattern of acquiescence, a dehumanizing reversal of ends and means, in all of their behavior. He finds it in their pretentious furnishings, their uncomfortable clothing, their grim factories, the dispirited way they eat and farm the land and work from dawn to dusk. He locates it, above all, in their economy—a system within which they work endlessly, not to reach a goal of their own choosing but to satisfy the demands of the market mechanism. The moral, in short, is that here "men have become the tools of their tools."

The omnipresence of tools, gadgets, instruments is symptomatic of the Concord way. Like Carlyle, Thoreau uses technological imagery to represent more than industrialization in the narrow, economic sense. It accompanies a mode of perception, an emergent system of meaning and value—a culture. In fact his overdrawn indictment of the Concord "economy" might have been written to document Carlyle's dark view of industrialism. Thoreau feels no simple-minded Luddite hostility toward the new inventions; they are, he says, "but improved means to an unimproved end. . . ." What he is attacking is the popular illusion that improving the means is enough, that if the machinery of society is put in good order (as Carlyle had said) "all were well with us; the rest would care for itself!" He is contending against a culture pervaded by this mechanistic outlook. It may well be conducive to material progress, but it also engenders deadly fatalism and despair. At the outset, then, Thoreau invokes the image of the machine to represent the whole tone and quality of Concord life or, to be more precise, anti-life:

> Actually, the laboring man has not leisure for a true integrity day by day; he cannot afford to sustain the manliest relations to men; his labor would be depreciated in the market. He has no time to be anything but a machine.

The clock, favorite "machine" of the Enlightenment, is a master machine in Thoreau's model of the capitalist economy. Its function is decisive because it links the industrial apparatus with consciousness. The laboring man becomes a machine in the sense that his life becomes more closely geared to an impersonal and seemingly autonomous system.[3] If the advent of power technology is alarming, it is because it occurs within this cultural context. When Thoreau depicts the machine as it functions within the Concord environment, accordingly, it is an instrument of oppression: "We do not ride upon the railroad; it rides upon us." But later, when seen from the Walden perspective, the railroad's significance becomes quite different.

Thoreau's denunciation of the Concord "economy" prefigures the complex version of the Sleepy Hollow episode in the fourth chapter, "Sounds." The previous chapter is about "Reading," or what he calls the language of metaphor. Now he shifts to sounds, "the language which all things and events speak without metaphor, which alone is copious and standard." The implication is that he is turning from the conventional language of art to the spontaneous language of nature. What concerns him is the hope of making the word one with the thing, the notion that the naked fact of sensation, if described with sufficient precision, can be made to yield its secret—its absolute meaning. This is another way of talking about the capacity of nature to "produce delight"—to supply value and meaning. It is the crux of transcendental pastoralism. Hence Thoreau begins with an account of magnificent summer days when, like Hawthorne at the Hollow, he does nothing but sit "rapt in a revery, amidst the pines and . . . sumachs, in undisturbed solitude and stillness." These days, unlike days in Concord, are not "minced into hours and fretted by the ticking of a clock." Here is another pastoral interlude, a celebration of idleness and that sense of relaxed solidarity with the universe that presumably comes with close attention to the language of nature. For a moment Thoreau allows us to imagine that he has escaped the clock, the Concord definition of time and, indeed, the dominion of the machine. But then, without raising his voice, he reports the "rattle of railroad cars" in the woods.

At first the sound is scarcely audible. Thoreau casually mentions it at the end of a long sentence in which he describes a series of sights and sounds: hawks circling the clearing, a tantivy of wild pigeons, a mink stealing out of the marsh, the sedge bending under the weight

---

[3] Thoreau's response to the mechanization of time reflects the heightened significance of the clock in the period of the "take-off" into full-scale industrialism. With the building of factories and railroads it became necessary, as never before, to provide the population with access to the exact time. This was made possible, in New England, by the transformation of the clockmaking industry. Before 1800 clocks had been relatively expensive luxury items made only by master craftsmen. Significantly enough, the industry was among the first to use machines and the principle of interchangeable part manufacture. By 1807, in Connecticut, Eli Terry had begun to produce wooden clocks in large numbers, and before he died in 1852 he was making between 10,000 and 12,000 clocks a year sold at $5.00 each.

of reedbirds, and then, as if belonging to the very tissue of nature: "and for the last half-hour I have heard the rattle of railroad cars, now dying away and then reviving like the beat of a partridge, conveying travellers from Boston to the country." It would have been difficult to contrive a quieter entrance, which may seem curious in view of the fact that Thoreau then devotes nine long paragraphs to the subject. Besides, he insists upon the importance of the Fitchburg Railroad in the Walden scene; it "touches the pond" near his house, and since he usually goes to the village along its causeway, he says, "I . . . am, as it were, related to society by this link." [4] And then, what may at first seem even more curious, he introduces the auditory image of the train a second time, and with a markedly different emphasis:

> The whistle of the locomotive penetrates my woods summer and winter, sounding like the scream of a hawk sailing over some farmer's yard, informing me that many restless city merchants are arriving within the circle of the town. . . .

Now the sound is more like a hawk than a partridge, and Thoreau playfully associates the hawk's rapacity with the train's distinctive mechanical cadence:

> All the Indian huckleberry hills are stripped, all the cranberry meadows are raked into the city. Up comes the cotton, down goes the woven cloth; up comes the silk, down goes the woollen; up come the books, but down goes the wit that writes them.

What are we to make of this double image of the railroad? First it is like a partridge, then a hawk; first it blends into the landscape like the industrial images in the Inness painting, but then, a moment later, it becomes the discordant machine of the Sleepy Hollow notes. What does the railroad signify here? On inspection the passage proves to be a sustained evocation of the ambiguous meaning of the machine and its relation to nature. Every significant image is yoked to an alternate:

> When I meet the engine with its train of cars moving off with planetary motion,—or, rather, like a comet . . .

Or the cloud of smoke

> . . . rising higher and higher, going to heaven while the cars are going

---

[4] It is significant that Thoreau added this statement, with its obvious claim for the symbolic significance of the railroad, to the version of the episode he had published earlier in *Sartain's Union Magazine*, XI (1852), 66-8.

to Boston, conceals the sun for a minute and casts my distant field into the shade. . . .

The point becomes explicit in a thought that Thoreau repeats like a refrain: "If all were as it seems, and men made the elements their servants for noble ends!"

The image of the railroad on the shore of the pond figures an ambiguity at the heart of *Walden*. Man-made power, the machine with its fire, smoke, and thunder, is juxtaposed to the waters of Walden, remarkable for their depth and purity and a matchless, indescribable color—now light blue, now green, almost always pellucid. The iron horse moves across the surface of the earth; the pond invites the eye below the surface. The contrast embodies both the hope and the fear aroused by the impending climax of America's encounter with wild nature. As Thoreau describes the event, both responses are plausible, and there is no way of knowing which of them history is more likely to confirm. Earlier he had made plain the danger of technological progress, and here at the pond it again distracts his attention from other, presumably more important, concerns. Yet he is elated by the presence of this wonderful invention. In Concord, within the dominion of the mechanistic philosophy, the machine rode upon men, but when seen undistorted from Walden, the promise of the new power seems to offset the danger. Thoreau is delighted by the electric atmosphere of the depot and the cheerful valor of the snow-plow crews. He admires the punctuality, the urge toward precision and order, the confidence, serenity, and adventurousness of the men who operate this commercial enterprise:

. . . when I hear the iron horse make the hills echo with his snort like thunder, shaking the earth with his feet, and breathing fire and smoke from his nostrils (what kind of winged horse or fiery dragon they will put into the new Mythology I don't know), it seems as if the earth had got a race now worthy to inhabit it. If all were as it seems, and men made the elements their servants for noble ends!

If the interrupted idyll represents a crucial ambiguity, it also represents at least one certainty. The certainty is change itself—the kind of accelerating change, or "progress," that Americans identify with their new inventions, especially the railroad. For Thoreau, like Melville's Ahab, this machine is the type and agent of an irreversible process: not mere scientific or technological development in the narrow sense, but the implacable advance of history. "We have constructed a fate," he writes, "an *Atropos,* that never turns aside. (Let that be the name of your engine.)" The episode demonstrates that the Walden site cannot provide a refuge, in any literal sense, from the

forces of change. Indeed, the presence of the machine in the woods
casts a shadow of doubt (the smoke of the locomotive puts Thoreau's
field in the shade) upon the Emersonian hope of extracting an answer
from nature. The doubt is implicit in the elaborately contrived
language used to compose this little event. Recall that Thoreau had
introduced the chapter on "Sounds" as an effort to wrest an extra-
literary meaning from natural facts; his alleged aim had been to
render sense perceptions with perfect precision in "the language
which all things and events speak without metaphor." What he
actually had done, however, was quite the reverse. To convey his
response to the sound of the railroad he had resorted to an unmis-
takably figurative, literary language. Few passages in *Walden* are more
transparently contrived or artful; it is as if the subject had compelled
Thoreau to admit a debt to Art as great, if not greater, than his debt
to Nature.

The most telling qualification of Emersonian optimism, however,
comes in the deceptively plain-spoken conclusion to the episode.
Emerson had affirmed the political as well as the religious value of the
pastoral impulse. When he spoke in his public voice (as in "The
Young American") he interpreted the nation's movement toward "nature" (signifying both a natural and a spiritual fact—both land and
landscape) as motion toward a new kind of technically advanced
yet rural society. In effect he was reaffirming the Jeffersonian hope of
embodying the pastoral dream in social institutions. But Thoreau,
abiding by his commitment to stand "right fronting and face to face
to a fact," takes another hard look at the sight of the machine in the
American landscape:

> And hark! here comes the cattle-train bearing the cattle of a thousand
> hills, sheepcots, stables, and cow-yards in the air, drovers with their sticks,
> and shepherd boys in the midst of their flocks, all but the mountain
> pastures, whirled along like leaves blown from the mountains by the
> September gales. The air is filled with the bleating of calves and sheep,
> and the hustling of oxen, as if a pastoral valley were going by. . . . A
> carload of drovers, too, in the midst, on a level with their droves now,
> their vocation gone, but still clinging to their useless sticks as their
> badge of office. . . . So is your pastoral life whirled past and away. But
> the bell rings, and I must get off the track and let the cars go by;—

> > What's the railroad to me?
> > I never go to see
> > Where it ends.
> > It fills a few hollows,
> > And makes banks for the swallows,
> > It sets the sand a-blowing,
> > And the blackberries a-growing.

but I cross it like a cart-path in the woods. I will not have my eyes put
out and my ears spoiled by its smoke and steam and hissing.

Compared to popular, sentimental pastoralism, or to Emerson's
well-turned evasions, there is a pleasing freshness about Thoreau's
cool clarity. He says that the pastoral way of life—pastoralism in the
literal, agrarian sense—is being whirled past and away. It is doomed.
And he has no use for the illusion that the *Atropos* can be stopped.
The first thing to do, then, the only sensible thing to do, is get off the
track. Not that one need resign oneself, like the men of Concord, to
the dominion of the mechanical philosophy. But how is the alternative to be defined? To answer the question had been the initial purpose of the Walden experiment; now its urgency is heightened by the
incursion of history. If he is to find an answer, the writer's first duty
is to protect his powers of perception. At this point Thoreau adopts
a testy, tight-lipped, uncompromising tone: "I will not have my eyes
put out and my ears spoiled by its smoke and steam and hissing."

* * *

At the same time, however, he carefully nurtures an awareness of
the railroad's presence in the Concord woods. (The account of the
interrupted idyll in "Sounds" is only the most dramatic of its many
appearances.) There is scarcely a chapter in which he does not mention seeing or hearing the engine, or walking "over the long causeway
made for the railroad through the meadows. . . ." When the crew
arrives to strip the ice from the pond, it is "with a peculiar shriek
from the locomotive." And Thoreau takes special pains to impress
us with the "cut" in the landscape made by the embankment. He
introduces the motif in the first chapter, after describing his initial
visit to the Walden site:

> . . . I came out on to the railroad, on my way home, its yellow sand-
> heap stretched away gleaming in the hazy atmosphere, and the rails
> shone in the spring sun . . .

And he returns to it in "The Ponds":

> That devilish Iron Horse, whose ear-rending neigh is heard throughout
> the town, has muddied the Boiling Spring with his foot, and he it is that
> has browsed off all the woods on Walden shore, that Trojan horse, with
> a thousand men in his belly, introduced by mercenary Greeks! Where is
> the country's champion, the Moore of Moore Hall, to meet him at the
> Deep Cut and thrust an avenging lance between the ribs of the bloated
> pest?

The Deep Cut is a wound inflicted upon the land by man's meddling,
aggressive, rational intellect, and it is not healed until the book's

climax, the resurgence of life in "Spring." By that point the organizing design of *Walden* has been made to conform to the design of nature itself; like Spenser's arrangement of his eclogues in *The Shep-
heardes Calender,* the sequence of Thoreau's final chapters follows
the sequence of months and seasons. This device affirms the possibility
of redemption from time, the movement away from Concord time,
defined by the clock, toward nature's time, the daily and seasonal
life cycle. It is also the movement that redeems machine power. In the
spring the ice, sand, and clay of the railroad causeway thaws. The
wet stuff flows down the banks, assumes myriad forms, and arouses
in Thoreau a delight approaching religious ecstasy. The event provides this parablemaker with his climactic trope: a visual image that
figures the realization of the pastoral ideal in the age of machines.

The description of the melting railroad bank is an intricately
orchestrated paean to the power of the imagination. Although the
sand remains mere sand, the warming influence of the sun causes it
to assume forms like lava, leaves, vines, coral, leopards' paws, birds'
feet, stalactites, blood vessels, brains, bowels, and excrement. It is a
pageant evoking the birth of life out of inorganic matter. Watching
the sandy rupture exhilarates Thoreau, affecting him as if, he says,
"I stood in the laboratory of the Artist who made the world and me,—
had come to where he was still at work, sporting on this bank, and
with excess of energy strewing his fresh designs about." The scene
illustrates the principle in all the operations of Nature: an urge
toward organization, form, design. Every detail confirms the endless
creation of new forms. Out of winter's frost comes spring; out of an
excrementous flow, newborn creatures; out of the landscape eroded
by men and machines, these forms of the molten earth. "There is
nothing inorganic." The sight inspires Thoreau with a sense of infinite possibility. "The very globe continually transcends and translates itself. . . ." And not only the earth, he says, "but the institutions upon it are plastic like clay in the hands of the potter."

Thoreau's study of the melting bank is a figurative restoration of
the form and unity severed by the mechanized forces of history. Out
of the ugly "cut" in the landscape he fashions an image of a new
beginning. Order, form, and meaning are restored, but it is a blatantly,
unequivocally figurative restoration. The whole force of the passage
arises from its extravagantly metaphoric, poetic, literary character. At
no point does Thoreau impute material reality to the notion of sand
being transformed into, say, leopards' paws. It assumes a form that
looks like leopards' paws, but the form exists only so far as it is perceived. The same may be said of his alternative to the Concord way.
Shortly after the episode of the thawing sand, the account of the coming of spring reaches a moment of "seemingly instantaneous" change.

A sudden influx of light fills his house; he looks out of the window, and where the day before there had been cold gray ice there lies the calm transparent pound; he hears a robin singing in the distance and honking geese flying low over the woods. It is spring. Its coming, says Thoreau, is "like the creation of Cosmos out of Chaos and the realization of the Golden Age."

This reaffirmation of the pastoral ideal is not at all like Emerson's prophecy, in "The Young American," of a time "when the whole land is a garden, and the people have grown up in the bowers of a paradise." By comparison, the findings of the Walden experiment seem the work of a tough, unillusioned empiricist. They are consistent with Thoreau's unsparing analysis of the Concord "economy" and with the knowledge that industrial progress is making nonsense of the popular notion of a "pastoral life." The melting of the bank and the coming of spring is only "like" a realization of the golden age. It is a poetic figure. In *Walden* Thoreau is clear, as Emerson seldom was, about the location of meaning and value. He is saying that it does not reside in the natural facts or in social institutions or in anything "out there," but in consciousness. It is a product of imaginative perception, of the analogy-perceiving, metaphor-making, mythopoeic power of the human mind. For Thoreau the realization of the golden age is, finally, a matter of private and, in fact, literary experience. Since it has nothing to do with the environment, with social institutions or material reality (any facts will melt if the heat of imaginative passion is sufficient), then the writer's physical location is of no great moment. At the end of the chapter on "Spring," accordingly, Thoreau suddenly drops the language of metaphor and reverts to a direct, matter-of-fact, referential idiom: "Thus was my first year's life in the woods completed; and the second year was similar to it. I finally left Walden September 6th, 1847."

There is a world of meaning in the casual tone. If the book ended here, indeed, one might conclude that Thoreau, like Prospero at the end of *The Tempest,* was absolutely confident about his impending return to society. (Concord is the Milan of *Walden.*) But the book does not end with "Spring." Thoreau finds it necessary to add a didactic conclusion, as if he did not fully trust the power of metaphor after all. And he betrays his uneasiness, finally, in the arrogance with which he announces his disdain for the common life:

I delight . . . not to live in this restless, nervous, bustling, trivial Nineteenth Century, but stand or sit thoughtfully while it goes by. What are men celebrating? They are all on a committee of arrangements, and hourly expect a speech from somebody. God is only the president of the day, and Webster is his orator.

In the end Thoreau restores the pastoral hope to its traditional location. He removes it from history, where it is manifestly unrealizable, and relocates it in literature, which is to say, in his own consciousness, in his craft, in *Walden*.

Henry Thoreau[1]

by E. B. White

May 6th is the saddest day in the year for us, as it is the day of
Thoreau's death—a grief from which we have not recovered. Henry
Thoreau has probably been more wildly misconstrued than any other
person of comparable literary stature. He got a reputation for being a
naturalist, and he was not much of a naturalist. He got a reputation
for being a hermit, and he was no hermit. He was a writer, is what he
was. Many regarded him as a poseur. He was a poseur, all right, but
the pose was struck not for other people to study but for *him* to study
—a brave and ingenious device for a creative person to adopt. He posed
for himself and was both artist and model, examining his own position
in relation to nature and society with the most patient and appre-
ciative care. "Walden" is so indigestible that many hungry people
abandon it because it makes them mildly sick, each sentence being an
anchovy spread, and the whole thing too salty and nourishing for one
sitting. Henry was torn all his days between two awful pulls—the
gnawing desire to change life, and the equally troublesome desire to
live it. This is the explanation of his excursion. He hated Negro
slavery and helped slaves escape, but he hated even more the self-
imposed bondage of men who hung chains about their necks simply
because it was the traditional way to live. Because of a few crotchety
remarks he made about the factory system and because of his essay
on civil disobedience, he is one of the early Americans now being
taken up by Marxists. But not even these hard-working Johnnies-come-
lately can pin him down; he subscribed to no economic system and
his convictions were strong but disorderly. What seemed so wrong to
him was less man's economy than man's puny spirit and man's strained
relationship with nature—which he regarded as a public scandal. Most
of the time he didn't want to do anything about anything—he wanted
to observe and to feel. "What demon possessed me that I behaved so
well?" he wrote—a sentence that is 100-proof anchovy. And when he
died he uttered the purest religious thought we ever heard. They asked

1 Title supplied by the editor.

From The New Yorker *(May 7, 1949), p. 23. Copyright © 1949, 1967 by The New*
Yorker Magazine Inc. Reprinted by permission of The New Yorker.

him whether he had made his peace with God and he replied, "I was not aware we had quarreled." He was the subtlest humorist of the nineteenth century, a most religious man, and was awake every moment. He never slept, except in bed at night.

Chronology of Important Dates

1817   Thoreau born at Concord, Mass., July 12. Kant, Schiller, Coleridge, Wordsworth, Goethe. W. C. Bryant, *Thanatopsis*. Washington Irving, *The Sketch Book*. J. F. Cooper, *The Spy*. Napoleon dies.

1833-37   Thoreau attends Harvard. Longfellow comes to Harvard. Emerson moves to Concord, John Audubon, *The Birds of America*. E. A. Poe, *Tamerlane and Other Poems*. Thomas Carlyle, *Sartor Resartus*. George Bancroft, *History of the United States*. Noah Webster's dictionary. Stephenson invents locomotive. Erie Canal opens. England abolishes slavery; abolition movement in U. S. begins.

1836   R. W. Emerson, *Nature*.

1837   Thoreau camps by Flint's Pond with Stearns Wheeler. R. W. Emerson, *The American Scholar*. Nathaniel Hawthorne, *Twice Told Tales*. Charles Dickens, *Oliver Twist*. Accession of Queen Victoria.

1839   Thoreau teaches school in Concord; makes voyage on Concord and Merrimac rivers. Alexis de Tocqueville, *Democracy in America*. R. H. Dana, *Two Years Before the Mast*. J. F. Cooper, *The Pathfinder*. Brook Farm utopian community.

1841-43   Thoreau moves into Emerson's house. Hawthorne comes to Old Manse in Concord. R. W. Emerson, *Essays*. Thomas Carlyle, *Heroes and Hero-Worship; Past and Present*. Charles Dickens, *American Notes*. William Prescott, *Conquest of Mexico*.

1845   Shanty frame raised at Walden Pond in company of Emerson, Channing, and others. Thoreau moves in on July 4. Margaret Fuller, *Woman in the Nineteenth Century*.

1846   Thoreau addresses Concord Lyceum: *Writings and Style of Thomas Carlyle*. First trip to Maine woods. Arrest and jail for refusing to pay taxes. Nathaniel Hawthorne, *Mosses from an Old Manse*. W. M. Thackeray, *Vanity Fair*.

1847   Concord Lyceum: *The History of Myself* and "Walden." Thoreau leaves Walden Pond September 6, and lives in Emerson's house during his tour of England. H. W. Longfellow, *Evangeline*. Emily Brontë, *Wuthering Heights*.

1848-53   Thoreau lectures on *The Rights and Duties of the Individual in Relation to Government*. Publishes *A Week on the Concord and Merrimac Rivers* and *Resistance to Civil Government*. Travels to Canada. Active in abolition work and helps fugitive slave escape to Canada. Karl Marx and Friedrich Engels, *Communist Manifesto*. James Russell Lowell, *A Fable for Critics*. F. Parkman, *The Oregon Trail*. Nathaniel Hawthorne, *The Scarlet Letter*. Herman Melville, *Moby Dick*. Harriet Beecher Stowe, *Uncle Tom's Cabin*. T. B. Macaulay, *History of England*. Gold discovered in California.

1853   Thoreau elected to the American Association for the Advancement of Science.

1854   Thoreau publishes *Walden*.

1855-62   Thoreau travels and surveys in New England, New Jersey, and New York. He meets Walt Whitman. He walks the length of Cape Cod. He meets John Brown and speaks repeatedly in his defense. He travels to Minnesota for his health, dying May 6, age 44. Walt Whitman, *Leaves of Grass*. Oliver Wendell Holmes, *The Autocrat of the Breakfast Table*. H. W. Longfellow, *Hiawatha* and *Miles Standish*. Gustave Flaubert, *Madame Bovary*. Charles Darwin, *The Origin of Species*.

Notes on the Editor and Contributors

RICHARD RULAND, the editor of this volume, has taught at Michigan, Yale, and Washington University in St. Louis. He has written on Kafka, Brecht, Longfellow, Melville, and Henry Adams, and is the author of *The Rediscovery of American Literature: Premises of Critical Taste, 1900-1940.*

GERRY BRENNER is Associate Professor of English and Assistant Chairman of the Department at Boise College, Idaho.

JOHN C. BRODERICK is Professor of English at Wake Forest College and specializes in American cultural history. He is the author of *Whitman the Poet.*

GRAY BURR has published poems in *Poetry* and *The New Yorker.*

REGINALD L. COOK, Professor of American Literature at Middlebury College, is the author of *The Concord Saunterer* and *Passage to Walden.*

FRANK DAVIDSON, Professor Emeritus of English at Indiana University, has written frequently on nineteenth-century American literature.

NORMAN FOERSTER was a pioneer in introducing the study of American literature into American university curricula. He is the author of *American Criticism, Nature in American Literature,* and *The American Scholar.*

DOUGLAS GRANT has taught at Edinburgh, Toronto, Leyden, and Brisbane. At present he holds the first Chair of American Literature in Great Britain (at the University of Leeds).

BRUCE KING, formerly of the University of Ibadan and Lecturer in English at Bristol University, is Professor of English at the University of Lagos, Nigeria.

PAUL LAUTER is Assistant Professor of English at Hobart and William Smith Colleges. He has written essays on Thoreau and Emerson, and is the author of *Theories of Comedy.*

LEO MARX teaches at Amherst, where he is Professor of English and American Studies. He is the author of *The Machine in the Garden: Technology and the Pastoral Ideal in America.*

F. O. MATTHIESSEN taught at Harvard. His works include *American Renaissance* and influential studies of Eliot, James, and Dreiser.

PERRY MILLER, until his recent death, was Professor of American Literature at Harvard. He is best known for his studies of New England Puritanism, *The New England Mind* and *Orthodoxy in Massachusetts.*

JOSEPH J. MOLDENHAUER is Associate Professor of English at the University of Texas, where he teaches American literature.

SHERMAN PAUL, Professor of English at the University of Iowa, is the author of *Emerson's Angle of Vision* and *The Shores of America.*

JOHN B. PICKARD, author of *John Greenleaf Whittier: An Introduction and Interpretation,* is Associate Professor of American Literature at the University of Florida.

CONSTANCE ROURKE was educated at the Sorbonne and Vassar, where she taught for several years. A specialist in the field of American popular culture, she wrote on folk heroes and various aspects of the American cultural past.

WILLIAM BYSSHE STEIN, Professor of English at Harpur College, is the author of *Hawthorne's Faust: A Study of the Devil Archetype.*

E. B. WHITE has been a regular contributor to *Harper's Magazine* and *The New Yorker.* He has written frequently on Thoreau.

Selected Bibliography

Canby, Henry S., *Thoreau*. Boston: Houghton Mifflin Co., 1939. The best modern biography available.

Harding, Walter, *A Thoreau Handbook*. New York: New York University Press, 1959. An introduction to Thoreau scholarship.

————, *Thoreau: A Century of Criticism*. Dallas: Southern Methodist University Press, 1954. Includes the important early assessments by Emerson, Lowell, and Stevenson.

Leary, Lewis, "Thoreau," in *Eight American Authors*, ed. Floyd Stovall. New York: New York University Press, 1956; W. W. Norton & Co., Inc., 1962. A fifty-four-page bibliographical essay.

Matthiessen, F. O., *American Renaissance*. New York: Oxford University Press, 1941. Still the best study of Transcendentalist aesthetics.

Paul, Sherman, *Shores of America: Thoreau's Inward Exploration*. Urbana, Ill.: University of Illinois Press, 1958. An important biography of Thoreau's spiritual and intellectual life.

————, *Thoreau: A Collection of Critical Essays*. Englewood Cliffs, N. J.: Prentice-Hall, Inc., 1962. Contains good essays on *Walden* by Stanley Edgar Hyman, William Drake, R. W. B. Lewis, and Sherman Paul.

Salt, Henry S., *The Life of Henry David Thoreau*. London: Richard Bentley, 1890; revised edition, Walter Scott, Ltd., 1896. Still valuable for its interpretive insights, though factually outdated.

Shanley, J. Lyndon, *The Making of Walden*. Chicago: University of Chicago Press, 1957. A detailed account of the stages in the composition of *Walden*.

Sherwin, Stephen, and Richard Reynolds, *Word-Index to Walden*. Charlottesville: University of Virginia Press, 1960. Useful for tracing themes and images or locating quotations.